D0369393

CAN THERE BE A PRIVATE LANGUAGE?

JANUA LINGUARUM

STUDIA MEMORIAE
NICOLAI VAN WIJK DEDICATA

edenda curat

C. H. VAN SCHOONEVELD

INDIANA UNIVERSITY

SERIES MINOR

100

1970

MOUTON

THE HAGUE · PARIS

CAN THERE BE A PRIVATE LANGUAGE?

AN EXAMINATION OF SOME PRINCIPAL ARGUMENTS

by

WARREN B. SMERUD

CONCORDIA COLLEGE, MOORHEAD

1970

MOUTON

THE HAGUE · PARIS

LIBRARY OF CONGRESS CATALOG CARD NUMBER: 73-126054

To Audrey, Peter and Carl

PREFACE

A number of arguments have been advanced by contemporary philosophers in support of the thesis that there can be no such thing as a private language. It is claimed by those who hold this view that from its truth important consequences follow which have relevance to such philosophic subject-matter as sense-data theory, phenomenalistic doctrines, and the 'problem of other minds'.

Initially the writer attempts to indicate the nature of the logical connection which the anti-private-language thesis has to the above-mentioned areas of philosophy.

Prior to an examination of some main arguments which have been advanced in support of the anti-private-language thesis, it is noted that, although the thesis in question is commonly attributed to Ludwig Wittgenstein, some persons have doubted that there exists a clear justification for so doing; the origin of the thesis is allowed to stand as an open question. The arguments examined in what follows are found in the publications of three philosophers who are currently active, namely Norman Malcolm, James D. Carney, and Newton Garver, all of whom regard the thesis as Wittgenstein's, and the arguments presented by themselves as essentially contained in relevant passages in Wittgenstein's *Philosophical Investigations*. It is not being claimed that all arguments which have been advanced in support of the anti-private-language thesis are under study, but only that the arguments being considered are those which have been most commonly advanced.[1]

1 Two arguments which are not treated in the present study are: the second argument sketched out by Moreland Perkins in "Two Arguments against a

The first argument considered is the claim that the supposition that one could keep a record of a particular kind of sensation having no publicly-observable behavioral or circumstantial indicators is unintelligible, this being so because (a) the user of the putative sensation-word would have no way of determining whether or not he was using the term consistently, and (b) in the absence of a 'way of finding out', a putative sensation-word could have no meaning, even for its ostensible user.

Some existing criticisms of (a) are reviewed, and it is concluded that a Cartesian sceptical approach to memory and recognition is required in order to render (a) plausible. In the course of the discussion of (a), two additional arguments for the anti-private-language thesis, the first involving a claim that the ostensible user of a private language could have no concept of 'correct use', and the second involving a similar claim with respect to 'sameness', are considered, and reasons are advanced for rejecting these arguments.

A recent argument that (b) depends upon a revised formulation of the Verification Principle is noted, and later is is argued that from accounts of the sensation-word-meaning relationship subscribed to by Malcolm, Garver and Carney, a variant of the Verifiability Principle can be deduced.

Another main argument which is considered, I have called the 'manometer argument'. This argument depends directly on the sensation-word-meaning account subscribed to by advocates of the anti-private-language thesis. In examining the argument, it is noted that a logical consequence of the sensation-word-meaning account on which it rests (which I have called 'the outward-criterion doctrine') is that the inverted-spectrum hypothesis, together with all simplified variants, must be dismissed on logical-conceptual

---

Private Language'', *Journal of Philosophy*, 62: 443-459 (1965), and an argument presented by P.F. Strawson in *Individuals: An Essay in Descriptive Metaphysics*, (London, Methuen, 1959). It is not implied that an examination of these arguments would not have been worthwhile; however, in the judgment of the writer, they deserve a treatment which would carry one considerably outside the scope of the material which follows.

grounds as unintelligible. It is then argued that the inverted-spectrum hypothesis is not conceptually incoherent, since existence of empirical evidence for an instantiation of transposed color-experience is a logical possibility, and therefore that the outward-criterion doctrine must be incorrect. Some anticipated objections, a 'change-of-criterion-change-of-meaning' objection, and a claim that the argument that empirical evidence for transposition of color-experiences is possible involves a defective concept of justification, are examined and rejected.

Finally, an alternative account of the sensation-word-meaning relationship is suggested. It is concluded that, if the set of arguments examined are taken as constituting all available support for the anti-private-language thesis, then the only sense in which the thesis can be held to be correct is one which is trivial and irrelevant to philosophy.

I wish to express my sincere appreciation to Robert J. Richman and James M. Smith, who read the earlier version of this manuscript and who offered many helpful suggestions and criticisms, and to Albert B. Anderson, who gave generously of his limited supply of uncommited time in reading and commenting upon both the earlier and the present, slightly revised, version.

Concordia College
Department of Philosophy
Moorhead, Minnesota

August 14, 1969   Warren Smerud

TABLE OF CONTENTS

I

INTRODUCTION

The claim that there can be no such thing as a private language is one which has received no little attention and a considerable degree of acceptance in contemporary philosophical circles. It is commonly held that this claim, which I, in this paper, will refer to as the 'anti-private-language thesis', was advanced by and is properly Wittgenstein's.[1] Further, it is claimed that the truth of the anti-private-language thesis is philosophically important.[2]

In this chapter I will first attempt to indicate the reasons for the philosophic importance of the anti-private-language thesis, that is, the importance of this claim provided that it is either true or sufficiently well-supported by cogent argument to warrant a reasonable doubt concerning its falsity. Second, the question as to what is meant by 'private language', in the claim that there can be no such thing as a private language, will be considered.

Subsequent chapters will be devoted to exposition and evaluation of some of the principal arguments which have been advanced in support of the claim in question and then to a consideration of the accounts of meaning and justification upon which, it will be argued, the thesis ultimately rests. An attempt will be made to show that the arguments advanced in support of this claim are inadequate to demonstrate its truth, and that the main arguments which have been advanced in its support depend upon (1) a Cartesian scepticism with respect to memory or (2) doctrines

[1] See below, p. 14f
[2] See below, p. 15ff

concerning meaning and justification which are vulnerable to serious objections. Finally I will attempt to indicate the sort of accounts which, in my judgment, are rationally preferable to those underlying the anti-private-language thesis.

Prior to indicating the reasons why the claim that there can be no such thing as a private language is, if true, of considerable philosophical importance, it is perhaps worth noting that, although the thesis being considered is generally credited to Wittgenstein, not all persons who are well-acquainted with Wittgenstein's later works agree that it is correct to attribute the claim in question to him.[3] In view of Wittgenstein's declarations to the effect that the advancement of theses and theories are not the proper business of philosophers, there seems to be some reason to take such an objection seriously.[4] One may suspect that a claim that Wittgenstein is the author of the anti-private-language thesis should be regarded with the sort of scepticism expressed by F.A. Siegler in response to another claim made on Wittgenstein's behalf:

Has Wittgenstein a logical theory? He disavows having any sort of theory at all. A doctor who makes a claim about having the measles should be taken seriously in his claim; and similarly the fact that Wittgenstein disavows any logical theory should lead one carefully to question assertions that he does have one.[5]

In any case the question as to whether or not there is sufficient warrant for the common assumption that Wittgenstein DID advance the anti-private-language thesis is not a question which I will attempt to decide here; it can, I believe, be set aside for the follow-

[3] See, e.g., some remarks on this point by Judith Jarvis Thomson in "Private Languages", *The American Philosophical Quarterly*, 1: 20 and 31, (1964). However, in most of those articles devoted wholly or in large part to the anti-private-language-thesis (see bibliography), the thesis is attributed to Wittgenstein.

[4] Ludwig Wittgenstein, *Philosophical Investigations* (New York, The Macmillan Company, 1953), Part I, sections 109 and 128.

[5] F.A. Siegler, "Comments" (on Newton Garver's "Wittgenstein on Criteria"), *Knowledge and Experience: Proceedings of the 1962 Oberlin Colloquium in Philosophy*, C.D. Rollins, ed. (University of Pittsburgh Press), 77.

ing reason: If it is the case that the truth of the claim that there can be no such thing as a private language entails important consequences for a number of philosophical problems and programs, then this thesis and its supporting arguments are of considerable philosophical importance apart from any questions of authorship.

However, it is hardly possible to avoid references to Wittgenstein's *Philosophical Investigations* in any extended discussion of the anti-private-language thesis, since those who have made the greatest effort toward presentation of arguments supporting this claim, as well as many who have advanced objections, have regarded the claim and its supporting arguments as essentially Wittgenstein's. In presenting some of the main arguments which have been advanced in support of the claim that there can be no such thing as a private language I will rely principally on three papers presenting arguments in support of this thesis, namely Norman Malcolm's 'Wittgenstein's *Philosophical Investigations*', James D. Carney's, 'Private Language: The Logic of Wittgenstein's Argument', and Newton Garver's 'Wittgenstein on Private Language'.[6] As is evident from the titles, all three purport to be presenting Wittgenstein's arguments for the claim in question. As indicated previously, I will not, in this paper, attempt to determine whether or not there is sufficient warrant for attributing the thesis to him. One will be in a better position to decide whether or not the thesis is in fact Wittgenstein's when some articulated alternative accounts of the relevant passages in the *Investigations* become available.[7]

Turning now to the claim that the anti-private-language thesis

---

[6] Norman Malcolm, "Wittgenstein's *Philosophical Investigations*", *The Philosophy of Mind*, V.C. Chappell, ed. (Englewood Cliffs, N.J., Prentice-Hall, 1962), pp. 74-100; James D. Carney, "Private Language: The Logic of Wittgenstein's Argument", *Mind*, 69: 560-565 (1960); Newton Garver, "Discusion:, Wittgenstein on Private Language", *Philosophy and Phenomenological Research* 20: 389-396 (1960).

[7] The greater portion of those passages most directly related to the private language controversy are contained in Part I, sections 243-270.

is philosophically important, the sort of significance which it is alleged to have is indicated by Norman Malcolm, who informs us that the possibility of a private language is presupposed in the formulation of a number of long-standing philosophical problems as well as in the sorts of attempts which have commonly been made to resolve them; for example, all traditional problems concerning inferring or constructing the external world, inferring the existence of other minds, phenomenalism, and sense-data theory, presuppose the possibility of the sort of language which the anti-private-language thesis denies.[8]

It is perhaps worth considering in some detail the logical relationship which the thesis has to the areas of philosophy cited by Malcolm. Malcolm does not spell out the relationship in explicit fashion; however, it appears plausible to suppose that, when spelled out in a rather rudimentary manner, the relationship is essentially of the following sort: There exists a body of philosophical theories, 'T', which depend for their intelligibility on the truth of certain presuppositions, 'P'. However, these presuppositions allow for the possibility of there being such a thing as a private language. If it can be shown that there can be no such thing as a private language, then presuppositions P are either false or in some important sense unintelligible, and consequently the body of theories, or whatever, denoted by 'T' are either false, basically unintelligible, or fundamentally misconceived.

I will now attempt to spell out the essential character of the elements which may be supposed to constitute P. The statements which follow are admittedly somewhat lacking in refinement; nevertheless it seems evident that anyone holding to the intelligibility of the problem of the external world or of other minds, or adhering to some sort of phenomenalism or sense-data theory, must accept propositions very much like them:

(p_1) For each person there is a realm of immediate sensory experience belonging to that person, examples being his experiences of color, his

---

8 Malcolm, "Wittgenstein's *Philosophical Investigations*", 75.

pains, and, in part, his dreams (if he has them); each person knows, or can know, what the elements of his immediate sensory experience are in a way which is different from the basis on which others infer or claim to know the sort of experience he is having.

(p_2) The connection between any element of immediate sensory experience and the behavior and circumstances on the basis of which others may ascribe that kind of immediate sensory experience to someone (e.g., a pain or the perception of a bluish color) is contingent rather than essential or conceptual; the MEANINGS of 'pain' and 'sees a bluish color' are not dependent on types of behavior and/or circumstances.

(p_3) There are words and linguistic expressions by means of which one is able to report and describe elements of his immediate sensory experience; a person employing these terms and expressions in reporting or describing elements of his immediate sensory experience is able to do so correctly only if that person has the capacity to distinguish one kind of immediate experience from another and to refer to elements of the same kind by the same words or expressions.

According to those who have advanced the anti-private-language thesis, the picture of the language-sensation relationship indicated above cannot be a correct picture, and is, in fact, radically misconceived, for if it were a correct picture a private language would be possible, and it can be shown that there can be no such private language. In showing that there can be no such thing as a private language, the presuppositions constituting the essential elements of P are shown to be untenable, and with the demise of P, all theories in class T are thereby interred with finality.

Should someone object that his formulation of sense-data theory, or any of the other theories which were consigned to class T, does not depend on the truth or intelligibility of p_1, p_2, and p_3, he is free to explain the reasons why his own theory or formulation of the problem in question is exempt; nevertheless it seems evident that many theories and problem-formulations of the general sort indicated by Malcolm do involve presuppositions essentially like those states in p_1, p_2, and p_3, and if this is so, AND the anti-private-language thesis has been shown to be true, then a result of considerable importance in philosophy has been achieved.

Prior to turning to the arguments which have been advanced in support of the thesis, it is worth noting what is intended by the expression 'private language' in this particular philosophical context, that is, what sort of a language it is whose possibility is being denied. Norman Malcolm informs us that 'By private language is meant one that not merely is not but CANNOT be understood by anyone but its speaker', the reason for this impossibility being that its words are supposed to 'refer to what can only be known to the person speaking; to his immediate private sensations[9].' Here Malcolm refers us to *Investigations* 243, a section in which Wittgenstein asks whether it is possible to imagine a language which would be 'private' to the person who uses it, in that

the individual words of this language are to refer to what can only be known to the person speaking; to his immediate private sensations. SO ANOTHER PERSON CANNOT UNDERSTAND THE LANGUAGE.[10]

Subsequently in his discussion Malcolm APPEARS TO add a stipulation to the notion of a private language which, if it IS intended as a preliminary stipulation, serves to render the concept of a private language extremely puzzling from the very beginning. However, prior to considering that matter, I want to suggest that Malcolm's INITIAL characterization of the private language whose possibility is to be denied contains an implication the nature of which is not altogether clear. The words of the private language are described as (1) having reference to what can only be known to the person speaking, and (2) as having reference to 'immediate private sensations', (1) and (2) being, one may suppose, different descriptions of the same referents. From the fact that the words have the type of referents indicated, apparently it is supposed to follow that the words of the language cannot be understood by others. One is justified in questioning whether the conclusion DOES follow, and if so, WHY the conclusion follows.

In connection with this question, James F. Thomson has made

9 Malcolm, "Wittgenstein's *Philosophical Investigations*", 74.
10 Emphasis is mine.

the following observation.[11] He notes that Carnap once held the view that if a thirsty man says 'Thirst now' and his statement is construed as referring to his sensations of thirst, it follows that what he says cannot be understood by his hearers, Carnap's conclusion being that, since such a sentence CAN be understood, it follows that "Thirst now" does not refer to the speaker's sensations but rather must be equivalent to some sentence or set of sentences about his body. On the supposition that some such belief may be the foundation for the implication indicated in *Investigations* 243, Thomson attempts to reconstruct the argument supporting Carnap's position:

Given (A) "If X says 'Thirst now' he says something which if true is made true by his having a sensation of thirst" and (B) "No one but X can know whether X has a sensation of thirst", it does not yet follow that (Z) "If X says 'Thirst now' no one else can understand what he says." We need some extra premises. It is a reasonable guess that Carnap would have offered something like (C) "It is possible for Y to understand a sentence only if it is possible for Y to come to know whether the truth-conditions of that sentence are fulfilled." (C is either a statement or a consequence of some statement of Verificationism.)[12]

Thomson suggests that perhaps Wittgenstein would have offered an argument similar to the above but with the words "immediate private sensation" replacing the word "sensation". But, he notes, a question arises concerning premise C:

Would Wittgenstein have offered Carnap's verificationist premise C? This may be doubted (at any rate it will be denied). But then what third premise are we to supply? For we still need one — for example a premise spelling out the notion of a sensation's being immediate and private.[13]

In addition to the question as to WHY it would be impossible for

---

[11] James F. Thomson, "Comments" (on H-N. Castaneda's "The Private-Language Argument"), *Knowledge and Experience: Proceedings of the 1962 Oberlin Colloquium in Philosophy,* C.D. Rollins, ed. (University of Pittsburgh Press), 119-124.
[12] *Idem,* "Comments" 121.
[13] *Idem,* "Comments" 122.

others to understand words referring to (1) what can only be known to the person speaking and/or (2) to immediate private sensations, there is a further question as to what sort of an impossibility (that others could understand) is involved in the hypothetical language.

Subsequent to his initial characterization of the private language, Malcolm informs us that a language which is really private would be one such that

it [would be] a LOGICAL impossibility that anyone else should understand it or should have any basis for knowing whether [its inventor and user was] using a particular name consistently.[14]

Although some persons have regarded the logical impossibility of understanding by others as being an essential element of a private language[15] (and indeed Malcolm does nothing to indicate that "logical impossibility" is NOT an INITIALLY postulated feature of the private language whose possibility is to be denied), as an initial stipulation, LOGICAL impossibility appears to render the entire enterprise of advancing arguments for the truth of the anti-private-language thesis superfluous, for as Malcolm subsequently remarks in the course of his discussion of Wittgenstein's use of the term 'criterion', it is logically possible that someone could be BORN with the knowledge of the meaning of a linguistic sign or that such knowledge could be produced in him by means of a drug.[16] So one might ask what possible reason could be given, if one accepts Malcolm's last remark, for its being a LOGICAL impossibility that anyone other than the inventor and user of the private language should come to understand it? I believe that the

---

[14] Malcolm, "Wittgenstein's *Philosophical Investigations*", 77. Neither Carney nor Garver explicitly state that a logical impossibility is involved. Garver does say that the question as to whether there could be a private language is NOT "the question whether there could be a language IN FACT used by only one person but CAPABLE of being understood by any explorer clever enough to see the connection between certain sounds (or marks) and certain circumstances." Garver, "Discussion" 389.

[15] E.g., Judith Thomson, "Private Language" 20.

[16] Malcolm, "Wittgenstein's *Philosophical Investigations*", 86.

answer to this question can only be provided by the conclusion of the arguments against a private language, namely that the putative signs of such a language could not have any meaning at all, even to their ostensible user, but then this is the conclusion which is to be established by the arguments for the anti-private-language thesis, and so it is difficult to see on what grounds LOGICAL impossibility is introduced prior to the conclusion of Malcolm's arguments.

Difficult though it is to obtain a clear view of what is to be meant by a private language, resolution of the question concerning logical impossibility is not, I want to suggest, essential to an evaluation of the arguments which have been advanced in support of the thesis. I will attempt to indicate why this is so: Malcolm, Garver and Carney are in agreement in the following respect, namely that notion of a private language has a hypothetical instantiation in *Investigations* 258, a passage in which Wittgenstein suggests that we consider the situation of a man resolving to record the occurrence of an 'immediate private sensation' through the use of a sign 'E,' the sign 'E' deriving its meaning by means of an 'inner ostensive definition' on the part of its inventor. A crucial element in this hypothetical situation is that others not only do not but CANNOT understand this putative sign 'E'. To the extent that arguments for the anti-private-language thesis hinge upon the stipulation that others have no way of coming to understand the alleged meaning of 'E', whatever force the arguments (supporting the claim that 'E' could not, in the postulated circumstances, acquire the intended meaning) have can be evaluated simply by (1) allowing as an element of the initial hypothesis, that, in the case of the hypothetical diary-keeper's 'E' there are NONE OF THE NORMAL METHODS, whether by observation of circumstances and behavior, or attempted explanation on the part of the user, or whatever, by means of which others will be able to come to an understanding of what the sign 'E' refers to, and (2) refraining from postulating any 'logical possibilities' of the sort mentioned by Malcolm in a subsequent discussion (i.e., being born with the knowledge or coming to understand by means of a drug). By taking

II

THE DIARY-KEEPER ARGUMENT

To procced with an exposition of one of the principal arguments for the anti-private-language thesis it may be useful to take as an example of the putative private language, the situation of the hypothetical diary-keeper sketched in *Investigations* 258.[1] We are to imagine the following: (1) A man wishes to keep a record of the recurrence of a particular kind of sensation. (2) The diary-keeper intends to use the letter 'E' to record the occurrence of this sensation. (3) The meaning of 'E' is to be fixed by his attending to a sensation of the type which he wishes to record, his concentration on the sensation constituting a sort of 'inner ostensive definition'. (4) The sensation is one which has no 'natural expression', i.e., we are to suppose that nothing in the diary-keeper's behavior (aside, one supposes, from the behavior involved in recording the sensation) will indicate the occurrence of the sensation. (5) Since others have no knowledge of what is being recorded by 'E', others cannot understand this putative sign 'E'.[2]

According to Malcolm, Garver and Carney, one way in which it can be shown that 'E' could not be used to keep any such record is to point out that the diary-keeper would have no acceptable means of distinguishing between correct and incorrect use of this putative sign. From this it follows that 'E' could not be a sign in (or the whole of) a private language, and the same considerations

---

[1] Ludwig Wittgenstein, *Philosophical Investigations* (New York, The Macmillan Company, 1953), Part I, section 258.
[2] That conditions four and five are elements of the situation is indicated in section 256.

would apply to any other putative sign in the same postulated circumstances.

Malcolm's version of this argument is perhaps the most well known.[3] Wittgenstein's diary-keeper is not specifically mentioned, but, in the example which Malcolm proposes (I fix my attention on a sensation and decide to call that kind of sensation 'pain' in the future), it is indicated that conditions of the sort specified in one through five above, with the exception of the desire to keep a record (1) are supposed to hold.

The private definition, Malcolm notes, will be a success only if subsequently the word is used correctly, 'correctly' here meaning consistently with one's initial definition. One is undertaking to call or refer to sensations of the same kind by the same word, and the initial definition will not be a success if the word is mistakenly applied to sensations of some other kind than the paradigm sensation attended to in the act of privately defining the term for oneself.

The difficulty with the case under consideration is that nothing exists which could serve as a standard or check whereby it could be determined that the word is or is not being used consistently, consistent usage being equated, evidently, with 'following a rule'. The user may be under the impression that he is following a rule, but what is necessary is that there be something INDEPENDENT of his impression that he is doing so:

The proof that I am following a rule must appeal to something INDE-PENDENT of my impression that I am. If in the nature of the case there cannot be such an appeal, then my private language does not have RULES, for the concept of a rule requires that there is a difference between "He is following a rule" and "He is under the impression that he is following a rule..."[4]

The above quotation, together with the claim that no appeal of the required sort is possible in the case of a private language, appears to

[3] Norman Malcolm, "Wittgenstein's *Philosophical Investigations*", *The Philosophy of Mind*, V.C. Chappell, ed. (Englewood Cliffs, N.J., Prentice-Hall, 1962), 74-81.
[4] Malcolm, "Wittgenstein's *Philosophical Investigations*", 76.

constitute the essential elements of Malcolm's argument.[5] If this is so, then what appears to be the bare outline of Malcolm's argument can be restated as follows: If 'E' is a sign in a language, then 'E' is governed by a rule. If something is a rule, then it is possible that one might violate it while believing one is following it. And, this possibility exists only if there can be an appeal to something which could prove that the rule is (or is not) being followed. But there is nothing of the required sort which can be appealed to. Therefore (by *modus tollens*) no possibility of unwitting violation, therefore no rule, and therefore no linguistic sign.

Newton Garver, utilizing the example of the diary-keeper in *Investigations* 256, presents a version of what purports to be the same argument which, unlike Malcolm's, does not explicitly mention the concept of a rule.[6] Garver's version runs as follows: The initial private ostensive definition must enable one in the diary-keeper's circumstances to apply the sign 'E' correctly each time However, it can be shown that such could not possibly be the case :.

... in the present case there is no criterion of correctness: because there could be no distinction between thinking you were right and being right we cannot speak of rightness here at all. [Reference to *Investigations* 258.] You cannot even BELIEVE you got the connection right (that, that sensation is the same one again); for you can only believe what can be true or false, and that the sensation is the same one again could not be determined to be true or false .... Since there is no criterion for saying that a sensation is that certain one again, you could not ... privately undertake always to use "E" for that certain sensation: the undertaking would be empty because you could never know whether you had fulfilled it or not [Reference to *Investigations* 263].[7]

In the general context of his article, it seems clear that by 'criterion of correctness' Garver means, as does Malcolm, some standard or means of checking, external to the subject's own impression that the sign 'E' is being used correctly, to which one could appeal in

[5] In the course of presenting the argument now being considered, Malcolm advances two claims which, in the interest of simplicity, will be considered separately. See below, page 40ff.
[6] Newton Garver, "Discussion: Wittgenstein on Private Language", *Philosophy and Phenomenological Research*, 20: 393f.
[7] Garver, "Discussion", 394.

order to determine whether or not the sign is being correctly applied. What follows from the absence of any such criterion is, according to the last sentence in the above quotation, that one could never KNOW whether he was applying the sign 'E' correctly. But evidently things are even worse than this, one cannot even HOPE that one is applying 'E' correctly; the lack of any independent check entails that any statement that 'E' is being used correctly is somehow WITHOUT MEANING. This is, I think, implicit in the second sentence. Since it cannot be determined that the sensation is the same one again, the statement that it is so must be without meaning and consequently can be neither true nor false.

If the above interpretation is correct, the logical bones of Garver's version can be stated as follows: If there is nothing independent of the user's impression that he is using the sign 'E' correctly that will prove that he is using it correctly, then the user cannot know that he is so using it (no possible criterion implies no possible knowledge). If there is in the nature of the case no way to know whether 'E' is used correctly, then the distinction between correct and incorrect application is meaningless (no possible knowledge implies no distinction between correct and incorrect). 'E' is a sign only if the distinction between 'correct' and 'incorrect' has application (no distinction between correct and incorrect implies 'E' cannot be a sign). There is (in the case of 'E') no possible criterion, therefore 'E' cannot be a sign.

A third version of what purports to be the same argument has been presented by James D. Carney.[8] In Carney's version, the argument is stated in a somewhat clearer fashion than one finds in the accounts given by Malcolm and Garver. Like Malcolm and Garver, Carney regards his formulation as being essentially a restatement of Wittgenstein's. Alluding to the diary-keeper in *Investigations* 258, Carney states that

he [Wittgenstein] maintains that in virtue of what we mean by "a sign's

---

[8] James D. Carney, "Private Languages: The Logic of Wittgenstein's Argument", *Mind*, 69: 560-563.

having meaning" the imagined situation is such as to exclude the possibility of 'E' acquiring a meaning.[9]

Carney bids us compare the situation of the hypothetical diary-keeper with that of a chemist who, on mixing X with Y, obtains a particular color and calls it 'C'. In the chemist's situation, there will be criteria for use of the sign 'C'. For example,

If one were uncertain whether a certain color is C, was not sure whether he used 'C' correctly, or wanted to determine whether he remembered C, he could ask someone, look on a color chart, mix X with Y, etc.[10]

Even if the criteria were IN FACT not available, it would still, in the case of the paint chemist, make sense to speak of correct and incorrect identification. Were the chemist to destroy the mixture accidently and fail to remember or record how the mixture was constituted, and then a week later identify a mixture as being colored C, the question as to whether he had correctly identified the color would 'make sense', but it would make sense only because we know how in other cases to find out whether a color word is used correctly:

... it is because we can in other circumstances determine whether a color word is used correctly, and because we can describe how we could have determined whether C was correctly identified, that it makes sense to speak of the paint chemist correctly or incorrectly identifying the color. If we could not make this distinction, then 'C' would be without meaning.[11]

Applied to the case of the diary-keeper, Carney's version is evidently something like the following: 'E' has meaning only if a distinction between correct and incorrect use makes sense. This distinction makes sense only if it is possible to determine whether some sensation which he calls 'E' is correctly identified. However, it is not possible to do so. Therefore, (by successive *modus tollens*) 'E' has no meaning.

One is justified, I believe, in holding that there is a fundamental

9   Carney, "Private Languages", 560.
10   Carney, "Private Languages", 561.
11   Carney, "Private Languages", 561f.

symmetry in these arguments presented by Malcolm, Garver and Carney. That there is enough symmetry to justify the claim that the three versions are variants of one and the same argument is something to which I propose to give some attention later.[12] For the moment let us assume that this is so and turn to a suggestion of Carney's as to what sorts of objections might be made to the argument. Carney writes that if one wishes to take issue with the argument there appear to be two alternatives. These are:

(1) Find a criterion of correctness in the diary-keeper's case. This means: identify that which makes it possible for the diary-keeper to distinguish between his thinking that he is using 'E' correctly and using 'E' correctly, correct memory of E and incorrect memory of E, etc. Or (2) show that a sign can have meaning without a criterion of correctness. This means: show that a sign can have a correct and incorrect use without there being any way of determining whether or not it is used correctly.[13]

I think that it is safe to say that many persons find that the conclusion of the argument runs counter to their own intuitions in the matter, for at the very least it does SEEM that there could be (and perhaps are?) sensations for which there were no natural behavioral indicators, and it is not unlikely that some persons would be inclined to believe that were THEY in the diary-keeper's situation THEY could invent a sign for a sensation of this sort and, with sufficient conscientious attention, keep an accurate record of its occurrences, the question of motivation to do so being admittedly another matter altogether. However, philosophically it is not sufficient to trust to one's own intuitions in the matter. If one is to attempt a reasoned rebuttal to the argument, it seems that the courses of objection indicated by Carney are appropriate ones. In the following chapter one of these indicated avenues will be explored.

---

[12] See below, p. 51ff.
[13] Carney, "Private Languages", 563.

III

ON CRITERIA OF CORRECTNESS
AND RELATED MATTERS

Consider the first avenue of objection proposed by Carney. One is to find a criterion of correctness in the diary-keeper's case. One must identify that which makes it possible for the diary-keeper to distinguish between applications of 'E' which appear to him to be correct and applications which are in fact correct.

Carney explicitly states that the criterion needed must be something which the diary-keeper himself can use, and it seems obvious that its employment must be thus restricted since, by hypothesis, others cannot understand the sign and so the possibility of correction by others must be ruled out.

Before proceeding, it may be well to note a question which may arise with respect to the term 'criterion'. One might suspect that 'criterion' is being used in some special and refined philosophical sense here, for it is believed by many, by 'Wittgensteinians' as well as others, that Wittgenstein employed this term in a special technical sense, a sense which must be understood if one is to come to some reasonably clear understanding of the *Blue and Brown Books* and the *Investigations*. However, I shall assume that the requirement is not that of finding something which will fit some special sense of 'criterion', first, because there is evidence that IF Wittgenstein employed the term 'criterion' in some special sense, some who should have expert knowledge of this special sense of the term have not succeeded in making this sense clear to others,[1] and second,

---

[1] See, for example, "Comments" by Carl Ginet, F.A. Siegler and Paul Ziff on Newton Garver's paper "Wittgenstein on Criteria", *Knowledge and Expe-*

there is a contrary (minority?) evaluation of the matter by persons of apparent competence that any attempt to establish that Wittgenstein did employ the term in some special technical sense is not well founded. To illustrate, we have Ziff's pungent comments on one such attempt to explicate the alleged special sense of the concept:

Mr. Garver wants to know what Wittgenstein meant by 'criterion'. Well, what's the problem? He meant by 'criterion' something like test, or standard or way of telling. That is, he meant what any speaker of his dialect would have meant if he were using the word in familiar ways. I am inclined to suppose that most likely his use of the word 'criterion' would fit his use of the word 'game', that is, one might be able to discern a family of cases.[2]

A third consideration is that Carney does not announce that it is a criterion in some special sense that is required. So suppose one takes the question as to whether or not there is a criterion of correctness available to the diary-keeper as simply being a question as to whether it is possible to indicate something which would make it possible for the diary-keeper to distinguish between correct uses of 'E' and uses which only seem to be correct.

Carney notes that Carl Wellman has proposed a type of check or test which might be held to constitute a criterion available to someone in the diary-keeper's situation.[3] Wellman states that,

If memory has some credibility, one can check on his use of a word which stands for a sensation. He can arrange to have similar and contrasting sensations and see what he would call them.[4]

This proposal Carney sees as a purported analogue to the means by which one might confirm one's identification of a particular color

---

rience: Proceedings of the 1962 Oberlin Colloquium in Philosophy, C.D. Rollins, ed. (University of Pittsburgh Press), 72-85.

2 Ziff, "Comments", 84.

3 James D. Carney, "Private Language: The Logic of Wittgenstein's Argument", *Mind*, 69: 562 (1960).

4 Carl Wellman, "Wittgenstein and the Egocentric Predicament", *Mind*, 68: 225 (1959).

by seeing it next to similar and contrasting colors. Carney makes the following objection:

> But ... the cases are not analogous, for the recognition of the color must be a correct recognition. And seeing the color next to others is not the highest court of appeal.[5]

The difference between the two cases, as Carney sees them, is apparently the following: In the case of colors, comparing the particular color in question with others might enable one to recognize that its particular shade IS, say, the same as the painted walls in one's living room (the paradigm), but the ULTIMATE TEST ("the highest court of appeal") would be to compare the color of the object in question with that of one's living room walls. An analogous appeal is not open to the diary-keeper, for the paradigm sensation (the one upon which he fixed his attention in his initial inner ostensive definition) is not similarly available.

However, it has not been obvious to everyone that the absence of such a paradigm constitutes a serious disability. Suppose, to take up Wellman's suggestion for a moment, that the hypothetical diary-keeper experiences a number of types of sensations (e.g., four) fitting the conditions one through five which were set out for E.[6] Could the subsequent occurence of, say, F, G, H or I, serve for him as some sort of means of 'checking' as to whether a prior identification of particular sensation as E was actually correct?

In his paper, "Can There Be a Private Language?"[7] A.J. Ayer argues that there is no reason to believe that checks of the sort suggested could not be of value. On Ayer's view this must be so because unless it is acknowledged that some of our recognitions may be taken as valid in themselves, there would be no possibility of checking on the correct use of ANY linguistic sign. Further, there is *a priori* no reason why, granted that one is warranted in believing some of one's 'public' recognitions to be correct, the likelihood of correct recognition of private sensations should not

5 Carney, "Private Language", 562
6 Above, p. 23.
7 A.J. Ayer, "Can There Be a Private Language?", *The Concept of a Person and Other Essays* (New York, St. Martin's Press, 1963), 1-51.

be conceded also; if checks are held to be needed in the case of private sensations, there is no reason to suppose that such recognitions could not support one another:

My argument is that since every process of checking must terminate in some act of recognition, no process of checking can establish anything unless some acts of recognition are taken as valid in themselves. This does not imply that these acts of recognition are uncheckable in the sense that their deliverances could not in turn be subjected to further checks; but then these further checks would have to terminate in acts of recognition which were valid in themselves and so on *ad infinitum*. If the inference drawn from this is that an act of recognition is worthless unless it is corroborated by other acts of recognition, the recognition of private sensations will not necessarily be excluded. For there is no reason in principle why such acts of recognition should not corroborate one another.[8]

Whatever degree of force one may find in Ayer's remarks, it is fairly clear that the checking of one sensation against another would not be acceptable procedure for either Malcolm, Garver or Carney. Objections to such a procedure would follow the lines of Malcolm's objection to any claim that the reliability of memory might be sufficient to furnish warrant for supposing that someone in a situation like that of the diary-keeper could make consistent application of a particular sign to instances of the same sensation. Malcolm's reply is that memory ultimately stands in need of the possibility of appealing to something independent of particular memories. Referring to the well-known passage in *Investigations* 265, Malcolm acknowledges that one might check one's memory of the time of departure of a train by visualizing how a page of the time-table looked, but this procedure would be of no value unless the mental image itself could be checked through actually looking at the time-table.[9] The *desideratum* is that there exist something

[8] Ayer, "Private Language?", 42. The quoted material constitutes a portion of a footnote added subsequent to this paper's initial appearance in the *Aristolelian Society Supplementary Volume* XXVIII (1954). Others have voiced the same objection, e.g., Carl Wellman, "Wittgenstein's Conception of a Criterion", *The Philosophical Review,* 71: 445ff. (1962).

[9] Norman Malcolm, "Wittgenstein's *Philosophical Investigations*", *The Philosophy of Mind,* V.C. Chappel, ed. (Englewood Cliffs, N.J., Prentice-Hall, 1962), 77.

independent of a subject's memories (i.e. his 'impressions' that something is the case) which could, at least in principle, be appealed to in order for one's memories to be allowed some weight in deciding any question of fact. It seems clear that occurrences of 'similar and contrasting sensations' are in a position analogous to the memory-image of the railway time-table; there is nothing comparable to the time-table, something NON-SUBJECTIVE, which could confirm with certainty that, say, "this one is an F, that one is a G", and so on, and so G, H, I and J lack the credentials essential to a legitimate role in corroborating the recognition of some other sensation as an E.

It is not difficult to see that Ayer's objection to the above will be that one's recognition and interpretation of the relevant material in the time-table is in itself something which is subject to error, and so appeal to this 'highest court' will not in itself guarantee freedom from error, and similarly if one attempts to confirm one's recognition by asking others what the time-table says, one is appealing to other fallible human beings, and even if the answer which others give are correct, one must understand their replies correctly, and remember the information correctly if it is to be of any value, and so on.

It would be quite natural and reasonable to object to the point that Ayer would be attempting to make on the grounds that some very unreasonable doubts are being proposed. After all the percentage of instances in which such errors, misrecognitions and the like are made with respect to railway time-tables is perhaps not very great, and granted that such errors do occur, a railway time-table has a degree of complexity which renders the likelihood of mistaken interpretation by oneself AND others some appearance of plausibility. It may be held that a better example would be a case having a more simple nature, such as checking as to whether this colored patch is an instance of the color 'C'. Now the 'highest court of appeal' is, let us suppose, a paradigm sample on a color chart; surely it is unreasonable to suppose that anything is likely to go wrong in such a situation.

But such a change of example would not obviate the point Ayer is attempting to make, for one arguing along the lines sketched by Ayer COULD reply, "But you will have to make the comparison correctly, which means you must correctly recognize the paradigm as the paradigm and not mistake something else for it, and further, supposing that you have correctly recognized the paradigm, if then it SEEMS to you that the color on the patch in question is not the same as that shown on the paradigm, when in actual fact it IS, then the paradigm will be of no help, for your judgment will be incorrect in spite of the paradigm on the chart." An advocate for Ayer COULD say something like the above and I think many of us would be inclined (not irrationally) to hold that the statement is true. But one has, I think, an equally strong (and not irrational) inclination to hold that in the case of the color 'C' any actual doubt would really be a groundless doubt if the checking were to be done under good observational conditions by anyone endowed with normal eyesight and of sufficient intelligence to have the relevant question in mind (i.e., "Is the color on this patch C?"). Ayer would, one supposes, agree that an actual doubt would be groundless, as would anyone, or almost anyone, else who considers the matter. But the question which is appropriate in return is: How well-grounded is the doubt that the diary-keeper could (correctly) recognize a recurrence of the 'immediate private sensation' which he decided to call 'E'?

In order to pursue this question further it is perhaps worthwhile to pay some attention to the respect in which the notions of memory and recognition may be held to be involved in the example of the hypothetical diary-keeper. It seems evident that if the argument being considered is to be at all intelligible, occurrences of sensation E are to be construed as instances of a KIND of something. If the diary-keeper is to distinguish instances of E from instances of other sensations he must recognize these instances as being of the same kind as the sensation which he, at the beginning of his project, decided was to be called 'E'. In the initial phase of the hypothetical diary-keeper's undertaking, correct recognition of E will be dependent on correct memory of what the paradigm sensation was like in THIS SENSE, namely that should he fail to remember correctly what the paradigm sensation was like, then he will not be able to recognize subsequent sensations as being sufficiently like[10] the paradigm to be counted as E.[11]

Some persons may object to any claim that recognition is involved in every case in which one is able to apply the correct name to an object, for it may be argued that the notion of recognition properly applies only in those situations in which there exists some real possibility of FAILURE to recognize. It may be more in accordance with common usage to say that, in the case of those ordinary objects with which one is perfectly familiar, one simply knows what they are and that to speak of recognition in such run-of-the-mill instances is to complicate the matter unnecessarily, and perhaps that such a complication is philosophically dangerous. In any case, I think that it is not necessary to resolve this matter conclusively in order to proceed with the present discussion, for it must be conceded, I think, that if the diary-keeper should FAIL to recognize a particular sensation as an occurrence of E, then he will not know what it is to be called.[12] So, even though it might be objected that he need not 'recognize' the E, it is at least evident that (1) it must not be the case that he FAILS to recognize it, and (2) if he should find

[10] The notion of being 'sufficiently like' the paradigm admittedly stands in need of some comment. See below, p. 43ff.

[11] I do not wish to imply that memory of a paradigm is involved in one's ordinary correct employment of learned 'kind-names'— a native speaker simply knows, e.g., that the bird in the tree is of a kind called "owls". However, initially the diary-keeper's situation seems to be somewhat different and to be more like that of a man who, upon encountering a bird which is strange to him, decides to call any subsequently encountered birds of that kind "owls". If, prior to encountering the next owl, he forgets what the characteristics of the 'paradigm bird' were, it seems obvious that he will not know that the second bird is of the kind he decided to call "owls".

[12] It may be appropriate, for the present discussion, to divide cases in which one is witness to what one has 'encountered' previously into three categories: (A) One is so familiar with the object or whatnot that one as a matter of course knows what it is. (No talk of 'recognition' here.) (B) The object is not of a kind excessively familiar but one recognizes what it is. (C) One does not know what the object is called because one FAILS to recognize it. Using 'E' correctly will be a case of either A or B. There is also, it may be noted, a meaning of 'recognition' in which one recognizes an object (knows that he has encountered

himself unable to remember correctly what kind of a sensation it was that he decided to call 'E', he WILL fail to recognize it as being of that kind, and hence will not KNOW what it is to be called.

It is, of course, a truism that human memory is fallible and a truism that, on occasion, people fail to recognize something with which they have had acquaintance at some time in the past. But there are, it is well to note, all kinds of cases, and in some types of cases failure of memory and misrecognition are far more common than in others. It is true, for example, that I could fail to recognize, say, my cat "Tulip", whom I see nearly every day, but this will only be the case if conditions of observation are unusual and poor, or if, unknown to me, someone has significantly altered the animal's appearance, or if circumstances are exceedingly distracting. On the other hand, if Tulip's appearance were in no way altered and if Tulip had jumped into my lap, and lighting conditions were reasonably normal, and I did not know what SORT of an animal this was, or what its name was, or that it belonged to me, it would be fair to say that an informed observer of such an event would quickly come to the conclusion that this case should be described pathologically rather than as an instance of normal human fallibility. Similarly one would not, I think, know what to make of it if, upon attempting to teach a normally intelligent first-grader to distinguish drawings of triangles from drawings of circles, one found that this otherwise normal child was constantly in need of assistance in distinguishing one from the other. One would have a problem for the child psychologist.

From the very general fact that in some circumstances people may misrecognize, misidentify or fail to pick out correctly some object in question, it does not follow that in a particular sub-set of circumstances there is a real possibility that a normal human being will fail to pick out or identify, say, a drawing of a triangle or the cat which he has owned for five years. To suppose that the

---

it previously) but fails to remember, or has never learned, what is it called. One may suppose this latter sort of recognition will be of little or no help to the diary-keeper. In what follows I am using the term 'recognition' to cover both A and B.

latter follows from the former is to commit a type of mistake which, as Kenneth Stern notes,[13] was pointed out by G.E. Moore in his paper, "Four Forms of Scepticism", a paper in which Moore presents the following illustration:

It is possible for a human being to be of the female sex. I am a human being, so it is possible (I do not know whether) I am of the female sex.[14]

However, it is proper to ask, if one allows the model of object and knower as appropriate in discussing the subject of sensations (Wittgensteinians would not so regard it, but the inappropriateness of such a model is something which arguments for the anti-private-language thesis are supposed to show), what it is about sensations that would place sensations in a category like that of, say, my cat in my lap or drawings of triangles placed in clear view rather than the case of some person known to me whom, for some plausible reason, I might fail to recognize. The answer is, I think, that, in the words of Mr. Brian Medlin, "there is very little to go wrong."[15] One might fail to recognize someone with whom one has had previous acquaintance because that person has lost a considerable amount of weight, has grown a beard and is disguising his voice, or he is too far away or the light is not good; that is, his physical appearance may have altered or the conditions of observation may be too unfavorable. There is, of course, a sense in which we may speak of a sensation altering, e.g., a sharp pain gradually becomes an ache, but then it IS an ache, not something else disguised as an ache as John might be disguised as Uncle Fred. Second, in the case of sensations there is not something analogous to 'conditions of observation' which promote misrecognition. It is true that an exciting event might cause one to lose awareness of the painful condition of one's foot or the ringing in one's ears, but it would be a sign of mental breakdown if such a distracting or

---

[13] Kenneth Stern, "Private Languages and Skepticism", *The Journal of Philosophy,* 60: 757f. (1963).

[14] G.E. Moore, "Four Forms of Scepticism", *Philosophical Papers* (New York, The Macmillan Company, 1959), 220.

[15] Brian Medlin, "Critical Notice: *The Concept of a Person and Other Essays*", *The Australasion Journal of Philosophy,* 42: 423 (1964).

exciting event were to cause the subject to believe that he was referring to the former by the expression "ringing in my ears" or the latter by "pain in my foot". In short, the cases in which memory and recognitions based on memory are prone to error are so far removed from those involving sensations that it is difficult to conceive how any good ground could be given for supposing that in the case of sensations normal human beings would be prone to error, in the absence of any extra-mental means of checking, with respect to knowledge of what kinds of sensations they happen to be having.[16]

However, even one who accepted the above-noted considerations as having some substantial weight might, at this point, advance the objection that these are only considerations which weigh against the thesis that ('memory-based')[17] recognitions of sensations would be, in the absence of the possibility of 'extra-mental' checks, intrinsically unreliable. It might be held that what is needed here is something more, namely a PROOF that such recognitions are intrinsically reliable. To my knowledge there is no such proof available. But there is I believe, some ground for holding that any request for such a proof would not, at bottom, be a reasonable request. In a discussion of this point, Stern has suggested (and I regard this suggestion as well worth consideration) that in matters of this kind the appropriate philosophical policy is that indicated by C.S. Peirce, in his admonition to refrain from pretending to doubt that which one does not really doubt in one's heart, an admonition which, Stern notes, is set out in more extended form in a paper by C.L. Stevenson:

It is typical of the Cartesian approach to philosophy to reverse our

---

[16]   There are cases in which a person's description may be lacking in PRECISION; e.g., I might tell the doctor that I have a "stabbing pain" when "throbbing pain" would be the more accurate expression. But this would be quite different from the total failure which would occur in referring to it as a "ringing in my ears". Note Malcolm's statement that an inner ostensive definition of 'pain' will fail if one subsequently applies the word to emotions. "Wittgenstein's *Philosophical Investigations*", 76.

[17]   Perhaps it should be noted that there is such a thing as recognizing something on the basis of a past or present DESCRIPTION given to one by someone else. This sort of recognition is not in question.

modern sense of justice, and to hold that all our ideas are guilty until proven innocent .... Most of us have come to distrust this procedure! We have learned that the initial proof of innocence is hard to find .... I see only one way out of this difficulty — that of dropping the Cartesian approach altogether and holding our idea innocent until proven guilty. I say this not to propound a categorical imperative, but to make an ordinary proposal — a proposal which simply emphasizes in philosophy a procedure that we have long taken for granted in science and in daily life.[18]

I want to suggest that this approach outlined by Stevenson is a reasonable one in the present case. If this approach is not a reasonable one and some general justification of memory is required, it must be admitted that the required justification will not be found here.

The general question which began the present discussion was whether or not it is possible to find a criterion of correctness in the diary-keeper's case, the criterion being

that which makes it possible for the diary-keeper to distinguish between his thinking he is using 'E' correctly and using 'E' correctly, correct memory of E and incorrect memory of E, etc.[19]

It is fair to say that nothing acceptable to Mssrs. Malcolm, Garver and Carney has been discovered. However, it has been argued that there is good reason to hold that the lack of something 'non-subjective' is not as serious as proponents of the anti-private-language thesis apparently believe, and this because (1) as Ayer has argued, unless some of our recognitions are acknowledged as valid in themselves, no putative process of checking can be of any value, and (2) no good reason has been given for supposing that the recognition of one's sensations is the sort of situation in which the possibility of a mistake is anything more than the barest of 'logical possibilities'. Therefore, for all that has been said so far, it has not I think, been shown that there is any serious disability in the diary-keeper's project. I might justifiably say of him, "He's

---

[18] C.L. Stevenson, "Some Relations Between Philosophy and the Study of Language", *Analysis,* 8 (1947-48), quoted by Stern, "Private Language and Skepticism", 756-757.
[19] Carney, "Private Language", 563.

a bright boy and I have confidence in him; it is highly likely that his record of the sensation will be accurate."

At this point it may be of value to compare the diary-keeper's situation with Mr. Carney's paint chemist in the hands of a mischievous (but reasonably benign) demon: Let us suppose that the paint chemist has made up a color sample of the color C and that he tacks the sample on one of the walls of the laboratory. Suppose that upon turning off the lights before leaving (he always leaves after dark) the patch, which was a sample of C, turns into (due to the demon's agency) a patch of glowing green (which is not C). When he turns the lights back on the patch becomes C again, lights off, glowing red, and so on. As a further condition, the demon will perform this feat only when the paint chemist is the sole person present. Further, if the paint chemist should attempt to photograph this phenomenon, the demon will fog the film; if glowing color samples are brought in, he will refrain from causing the phenomenon in question, etc. In short, the paint chemist will have available to him no criterion of correctness in the sense which Mr. Carney (and other proponents of the anti-private-language thesis) indicate. Now assuming the paint chemist remains calm in the situation described, and that he desires to keep a record of the various glowing colors which appear, there seems to be no good reason to suppose that he will not be able to keep an accurate record. By parity of situation, since there is no good reason for supposing the paint chemist's record would not be accurate, there is no good reason for supposing that the diary-keeper would fail in his essentially similar undertaking.

Malcolm has at least two objections to assimilating the two cases in the above manner, one of which I find to be rather curious. The concept of correct use CANNOT, it would seem, apply to the diary-keeper's employment of 'E' for the following reason:

The notion of a private language doesn't allow that my behavior and circumstances can be so related to my utterance of the word that another person, by noting my behavior and circumstances, can discover that my use of the word is correct or incorrect. Can I discover this for myself, and how do I do it? That discovery would suppose that I have a conception of correct use which comes from outside my private language and against which I measure the latter. IF THIS WERE ADMITTED, THE PRIVATE LANGUAGE WOULD LOSE ITS PRIVACY AND ITS POINT.[20]

In reply to this several things may be said. First the diary-keeper example becomes unintelligible from the beginning, for one would in all fairness be obliged to postulate a sixth condition, namely that the diary-keeper has no conception of the correct use of a linguistic sign. All would agree that the entire notion of keeping any sort of a record is thereby made unintelligible. But then the whole matter (if it can be called anything at all) becomes devoid of any interest whatsoever. If the diary-keeper example is to be of any interest at all it must, it seems obvious, be assumed that this hypothetical figure has a conception of correct and incorrect use of signs employed in referring to kinds of things such as dogs, cats and tables; what is at issue is whether the diary-keeper could invent a sign to refer to a kind of thing which can be known to himself alone, and use this sign to keep a record of that particular whatnot in the absence of any extra-mental means of finding out whether he is applying the sign 'E' consistently. In the above remarks Malcolm has done too much, not with the same sort of result as the alleged admirer of Heraclitus whose effort to improve the Heraclitian thesis transformed it into its opposite,[21] but nevertheless with something that renders all discussion of the matter unintelligible. If the idea of a private language is to be allowed 'a fair run' (to borrow an appropriate expression from Castaneda) it seems reasonable to dismiss this objection as a self-defeating stipulation.

There is, however, a second and related objection which is deserving of some attention. Immediately prior to the above objection Malcolm writes:

If I recognize that my mental image is the 'same' as the one I had

---

[20] Malcolm, "Wittgenstein's *Philosophical Investigations*", 80. Emphasis is mine.

[21] A favorite example of Kierkegaard's. The disciple attempted to make the thesis stronger by holding that not only was it impossible to step into the same river twice, one could not even do it once. Aristotle, *Metaphysics,* 1010a.

previously, how am I to know that this public word 'same' describes what I recognize? [The following is a quote from *Investigations* 378] "Only if I can express my recognition in some other way, and if it is possible for someone to teach me that 'same' is the correct word here."[22]

Malcolm's objection is, I shall attempt to show, exceedingly weak, if anything, when applied to the diary-keeper. It is true that things may be the same in one or many respects and not be the same in others, and whether or not two things, objects, situations or what-nots are to be characterized as the same will depend, in a given situation on all sorts of relevant considerations; one cannot, I think, give a general recipe for relevance. More to the point, it is true that in a great many situations, there are what one might call accepted conventions for what counts as 'the same' and that in such cases there is a conventional correct employment of the word "same" which can be taught. However, the mental image example is rather interesting, for it is not at all clearly evident that the use of 'same' with respect to mental images need be governed by any precise sort of convention.

Suppose that Pat is a native speaker of English who, for one reason or another has no preconceptions about the word 'same' as applied to mental images; perhaps he has experienced very little mental imagery subsequent to his mastery of the language. Suppose Mike, the experimental psychologist, has a new drug he wants to test which he suspects will produce imagery. The psychologist believes that when given to the same subject at different times under conditions X, Y, and Z, the imagery produced at one time will resemble that produced at a subsequent time. So an injection of the drug is given at t_1 and another is given at t_2. Mike asks, "Did the injections produce mental images?" Pat replies, "Yes, on both occasions I had a vivid mental image of an elephant." "So you had the same image both times?" "I don't know whether to call them the same because the first image was of a pink elephant while the one following the second injection was of a blue elephant." The example can be complicated to any length one desires, but the

---

[22]   Malcolm, "Wittgenstein's *Philosophical Investigations*", 80.

above is perhaps sufficient. Whether or not the two images are to be regarded as 'the same' will in this case depend on the degree and kinds of similarity important TO THE PSYCHOLOGIST. In a sense Mike can 'teach' Pat that 'same' is the correct word here, but whether or not 'same' is to be the correct word depends on what Mike will regard as relevant. (It is not implied that his decision will be of a non-rational nature—one is free to suppose that Mike will have reasons.) Whether or not the word 'same' correctly applies will not, we may assume, be decided by taking a census of native speakers. Rather, the psychologist himself will, one is free to suppose, set some sort of limit for what is to be regarded as the same. He may decide that if an image is of the same kind of animal this will be sufficient for its being counted as the same and he may not. In any case he will not be teaching Pat some well-defined public use of "same" as it applies to images of elephants. Rather, he will be setting his own limits (for reasons of his own) on what is to count as the same.

This is of interest because we have in the case of the hypothetical psychologist, Mike, a situation which is in an important respect analogous to that of the hypothetical diary-keeper. No one can teach the diary-keeper the 'correct' use of 'same' with respect to his 'immediate private sensations', and no one will be teaching the psychologist the 'correct' use of 'same' with respect to the imagery of his experimental subjects. The psychologist will have to set his own limits, and it is obvious (since by hypothesis no one can teach him) that the diary-keeper must set his own limits if the sign 'E' is to have any consistent application.

It is perfectly proper to raise a question at this point, namely, how DOES the diary-keeper, in his situation, set these limits? Supposedly 'E' is to be used to refer to and record sensations of the same kind as the sensation upon which he fixed his attention at the moment of inner ostensive definition, but how it is that this sort of definition should suffice to determine his subsequent use of the sign may well have the appearance of a mystery. How can he pick out a KIND of sensation in so doing?

In her paper "Private Langugaes", Judith Jarvis Thomson

argues that whatever difficulties one may find in the above situation are not peculiar to it, but rather hold, in the absence of some doctrine having application only to sensations, for 'public' objects as well:

WHY any more trouble about picking out a kind of sensation than about picking out a kind of THING? Suppose I were to set about introducing by an ostensive definition a new name for a kind of ... squiggle I would like to pick out. I write a capital letter E on a bit of paper, and I say, that and any others of the same kind are to be called 'E's'. Have I picked out a kind of squiggle? Well, what other marks would be of the same kind? Would an italicized capital E be of the same kind? Or one with a long middle bar? Suppose when asked I said, "Yes, they are of the same kind", or, "No, they are not of the same kind." Need I have had them specifically in my mind when I introduced the kind-name 'E' in order for it to be the case that I was indeed picking out a kind of squiggle? Surely not. Or better, if anything of this sort WERE necessary if I were to have picked out a kind of thing, then it could have been present when I picked out a kind of sensation ....[23]

The above remarks appear to constitute a perfectly cogent observation; to obviate the above, proponents of the anti-private-language thesis would have to show why the situation of a newly-invented word for an 'immediate private sensation' is in a position inferior to that of a newly-invented word for some other sort of whatnot which one might want to pick out.

Thus far only the first avenue of approach suggested by Mr. Carney has been considered. It is to the second that I now wish to turn, namely to some considerations relating to his suggestion that one might attempt to show that a sign can have meaning without there being a 'criterion of correctness'.[24]

[23] Judith Jarvis Thomson, "Private Languages", *The American Philosophical Quarterly,* 1: 26 (1964).

[24] I regret that during the time in which this chapter was being composed I was unaware of the existence of Michael A.G. Stocker's excellent paper, "Memory and the Private Language Argument" (*Philosophical Quarterly,* 16: 47-53 [1966]); Stocker's discussion contains a number of points which should be of interest to anyone concerned with the issues which have been touched upon here.

IV

A RECENT INTERPRETATION
OF THE CRITERION REQUIREMENT

It has been noted that Carney suggests a second avenue of objection to the anti-private-language thesis, this being that of showing that a sign can have meaning without there being any way of finding out whether or not it is used correctly. First, it may be remarked, in passing, that one might take issue with this suggestion in that it could be objected that the burden of proof is on the proponents of the anti-private-language thesis, and that all that can reasonably be required of any objector is to point out that the claim that the existence ('in principle' at least) of a 'way of finding out' is a necessary condition for a sign's having meaning is open to reasonable objection.

In any case, it may be in order to examine somewhat more closely than has been done so far, the nature of this claim that a way of finding out is essential to a sign's having meaning.

In her paper, "Private Languages", Judith Jarvis Thomson presents an interesting version of what the claim that there must be a way of finding out in substance amounts to. It should be noted that in her paper Mrs. Thomson examines only Malcolm's version of the argument, so for the present one may leave it an open question whether there are features in the presentations by Garver and Carney which could not be assimilated to her examination of what she refers to as "Malcolm's thesis[1]".

Prior to sketching out Mrs. Thomson's version of the logical structure of Malcolm's version of the argument, it should be noted

[1] Judith Jarvis Thomson, "Private Languages", *The American Philosophical Quarterly*, 1: 20 (1964).

that Mrs. Thomson regards Malcom's thesis as being a claim that there can be no such thing as a language which LOGICALLY "could not" be understood by anyone other than its inventor and user.[2] As was previously noted, any formulation of the anti-private-language thesis in terms of logical impossibility seems to involve something rather curious in that the claim thus formulated appears to be reducible to an assertion which is completely trivial, namely to the statement that there can be no such thing as a meaningless language.[3] However, I believe that, once again, the vexing matter of LOGICAL impossibility can be set aside for the moment. In a subsequent discussion I will attempt to show that the soundness of the anti-private-language thesis depends upon the soundness of a certain view concerning the sensation-word-meaning relationship, and that this account upon which the thesis is dependent, if correct, would serve to show that from the absence of any normal means of coming to understand the meaning of a putative sensation-word, it follows that there can be no extraordinary means (e.g., a drug, or being born with such knowledge) either; that is, that if there are NO NORMAL MEANS then there can be NO LOGICALLY POSSIBLE MEANS.[4]

Mrs. Thomson finds three steps necessary to Malcolm's argument, the first of these being as follows: If a sign is to be a word in a language, one's use of the sign must be governed by a rule. This means that it must be possible to use the sign INCORRECTLY, that is, to fail to follow, or act in accordance with the rule. "For R is not a rule unless it is possible either to follow or to violate it."[5] Since Malcolm, she finds, does little to clarify the notion of a linguistic rule, Mrs. Thomson proposes a formulation of a linguistic rule governing a name of a kind of thing, formulation of the rule involving the mention of a sign, 'K' and of a kind of thing, the X's, the rule being that X's and only X's are to be called 'K's'. This done, the first step of the argument can be stated as follows:

2 Thomson, "Private Languages", 20.
3 See above, p. 20f.
4 See below, p. 97ff.
5 Thomson, "Private Languages", 22.

If a sign 'K' which a man uses is to be a name of a kind of thing in a language, his use of it must be governed by a rule of the form, X's and only X's are to be called 'K's.[6]

In order to keep the diary-keeper example well in mind, it is worth noting what the X's will be in his situation. An X for the diary-keeper will be a sensation of the same kind as the one upon which he fixed his attention in his initial ostensive definition. 'X' may be replaced by 'sensation of the same kind as that one'.

The second step of Malcolm's argument is, in Mrs. Thomson's judgment, a second condition on rules. That is, if R is to be a rule, it must (1) not only be possible to violate it, but (2) it must be possible to violate it UNWITTINGLY. From the fact that a man thinks that he is following a rule, it must not follow that he really is following it, this being ESSENTIAL according to Malcolm, to the concept of a rule.[7] Further, she notes, it seems evident that a slip of the tongue or of one's pen would not be the kind of violation required, for, since it is always possible that one might make a slip of this kind, no sign which one might use would be such that one's use of it would fail to meet this condition. This being so, Mrs. Thomson concludes that the sort of mistake the possibility of which is being required must be that of calling something "K" thinking it is an X when it is not an X. So the second step of the argument may be stated in the following way:

If a sign 'K' which a man uses is to be a kind-name in a language, then it must be possible that he should call a thing 'K' thinking it is an X when it is not an X, when it is the X's and only the X's which (in his use) are to be called 'K's'.[8]

The above requirements, she remarks, seems to be reasonable ones, but any claim that this second condition follows as a matter of course from the concept 'rule' itself is open to serious question, for it seems that one can find examples of rules which COULD NOT be violated unwittingly, and even a rule which could not be

---

6 "Private Languages", 23. Thomson notes that the notion of 'call' (in this context) is somewhat obscure.
7 Thomson, "Private Languages", 23.
8 Thomson, "Private Languages", 24.

violated knowingly. Since her discussion of her examples is quite compact, I am presenting one such example verbatim:

Suppose Mummy writes "Whenever you feel the least bit gloomy, think of your Mummy. (It will cheer you up.)" Could I think I was following this rule and not be? (Of course it may be said that it is not possible — knowingly at all events — to violate this rule, so that it does not satisfy the first condition on rules which was set out in step one of the argument. But then surely the possibility of something like this should rather show either that step one is not true for all rules, OR that, while one must be able to violate a rule if it is to be a rule, it is not required that one be able to violate it knowingly. And in fact things are really even worse than this. For notice that one can't even violate this rule unwittingly unless one has, in a sense, forgotten the rule. And now what rules — however private — can't be 'violated' in that way? ...).[9]

Supposing, however, that one's questions concerning step two (and step one) of the argument are set aside, it is evident, she notes, that in steps one and two by themselves nothing has been said which would rule out the possibility of a private language. Nothing has been said which rules out the possibility that the diary-keeper is keeping a record of a particular kind of sensation through his use of the sign 'E'. The diary-keeper could agree with the conditions set out in step one and step two and yet object that it does not follow from the fact that the sensation denoted by 'E' has no natural behavioral manifestations (i.e., is 'strongly private') that there is no difference between a sensation's being of the kind he had decided to call 'E' and its seeming to him to be of that kind.

If the argument is to succeed, Mrs. Thomson finds a third step required, a step which must be essentially the following:

There is no such thing as a man's thinking a thing is of a kind to be called

---

[9] Thomson, "Private Languages", 24. In his paper, "Meaning, Identification, and Other Minds", *The Australasian Journal of Philosophy,* 42: 383 (1964). J.W. Meiland proposes a rule which, applied to the diary-keeper case (Meiland does not use the diary-keeper example), would be something like the following: You may call any sensation 'E' which SEEMS to you to be like the paradigm sensation, and you may not call any sensation 'E' which does not seem to you to be like the paradigm. Here one has a linguistic rule which one could not be violating while believing oneself to be following it, unless one were simply mistaken as to what the rule said.

'K' and its not being so unless it is logically possible that it be FOUND OUT that it is not so.[10]

One then can show that 'E' cannot be a kind-name if it is shown that it is not logically possible that either the diary-keeper or others are able to find out. This is accomplished in two ways: First, by hypothesis there are, in the case of E, no behavioral indicators which would give others, or the diary-keeper himself, any good reason for believing that the sensation is of the kind to be called 'E', and second, the diary-keeper's later impressions that he was or wasn't mistaken are ruled out as being a way of finding out. So, it is not possible to find out whether 'E' is or is not being used correctly, and so 'E' is not a kind-name in a man's language.[11]

A question at this point is whether or not the third step set out by Mrs. Thomson IS contained in Malcolm's account. That such is the case, she notes, may be denied, for it is not set out explicitly. What one has are suggestions of the third step in queries such as,

Now how is it to be decided whether I have used the word consistently? What will be the difference between my having used it consistently and its SEEMING to me that I have? Or has this distinction vanished?

Unless, she notes, "Malcolm is taking it that, where it is not possible to 'decide' whether I have used the word consistently the distinction between my having used it consistently and its seeming to me that I have HAS vanished, then this passage is simply incom-

---

[10] Thomson, "Private Languages", 26. Emphasis mine. There is a question as to what kind of "finding out" is required here, that is must it be logically possible to establish that a thing is or is not of the relevant kind ("strong finding out")? Or would it be sufficient that it be logically possible that one could have good reasons ("weak finding out")? Mrs. Thomson concludes that it is "strong finding out" that is required. For her discussion of this point see. p. 28.

[11] One may question whether conditions described are sufficient to yield a LOGICAL impossibility. Is it logically possible that one could come to know that 'E' is being used correctly through the taking of a drug, for example? I am not certain the notion of such a thing happening is intelligible. In any case the conditions mentioned do yield the fact that no normal means of finding out are available. If this is all that is entailed, then a revision of step three is required.

prehensible."[12] Further, one has a passage following shortly after, "My impression that I follow a rule does not confirm that I follow a rule unless there can be something that will prove my impression correct", which, in her judgment, it is reasonable to take as a more explicit statement of the same point. In any case, if step three is not contained in the argument, "the argument simply stops dead in its tracks."[13]

I want to delay, for the moment, any discussion as to whether or not the above IS a correct rendering of Malcolm's argument (or Garver's or Garney's), in order to point to some rather interesting conclusions which are drawn in Mrs. Thomson's paper. What one ends up with is, in sum, something like the following:

A sign 'K' is not a kind name in a language unless it is possible to find out that something is or is not a K.

If this is what we have, then, she concludes,

... it is plain that it is nothing more than a revised formulation of something very familiar indeed, namely the Principle of Verification. We are no longer to say that what purports to be a kind-name 'K' has meaning if and only if it is possible to find out whether or not a thing is a K. But we are instead to say that what purports to be a kind-name 'K' is a kind-name in a man's language only if it is possible to find out whether or not a thing is a K. ... And the change then amounts to this: from "if and only if" to "only if"; and from "is meaningless" to "is not a kind-name in a man's language". Perhaps the reasons why this might not be thought to be much of an improvement will not need to be set forth.[14]

One has then, on Mrs. Thomson's interpretation, a revised form of the Verification Principle. Interestingly enough, she notes, this reformulated principle has no essential connection to the subject of sensations. Rather, this principle can be applied to any metaphysical problem concerning which there exists such a thing as a SCEPTICAL VIEW, for example, the metaphysical problem concerning the existence of material objects. Supposing that a sceptic were correct in holding that it is not possible that anyone could

---

12 Thomson, "Private Languages", 27.
13 Thomson, "Private Languages", 27.
14 Thomson, "Private Languages", 29.

know of any term which supposedly stands for a material object that it really applies to that thing, e.g., that although it may SEEM to one that there is a table in the next room, there is no such thing as KNOWING that there is one, nor even any such thing as having a good reason for thinking there is one, it will follow that words purporting to stand for physical objects, such as the word 'table', will have the same status as the diary-keeper's 'E':

All that is needed for turning a class of sentences 'S' into sentences of a private language is that whatever it is which is a way of finding out whether or not sentences of kind S are true should be made logically irrelevant to the truth of sentences of kind S. INSTANTLY it is not possible that we should know whether or not any sentences of kind S are true; and INSTANTLY if any man uses sentences of kind S it is not possible that we should know what he means by them.[15]

So far as I am able to discern, the above conclusion does follow if one accepts the argument as formulated by Mrs. Thomson, and it is perhaps a reasonable conjecture that Malcolm did not foresee the applicability of the general argument to terms standing for things other than sensations. However, it may be objected that Mrs. Thomson has not presented a correct rendering of Malcolm's argument. Before turning to that matter, I intend to consider for a moment another question, namely whether it is at least equally plausible to interpret the versions of the argument presented by Garver and Carney in the same way.

Carney, it has been noted, does not make explicit use of the notion of a linguistic rule. However, one is warranted, I think, in holding that there is an intended equivalence between using a sign correctly, which is the notion employed by Carney, and using a sign in accordance with a rule, which Malcolm seems to prefer. An equivalent to Mrs. Thomson's 'first step' is rather clearly indicated. It is indicated in a number of passages but is perhaps most explicit in a passage which has not thus far been cited. Subsequent to the passages quoted previously, Carney considers (and rejects) some suggestions as to possible criteria of correctness in the diary-keeper case. Suppose someone proposes that the

15 Thomson, "Private Languages", 30.

criterion will simply be what the diary-keeper says, i.e., if the diary-keeper says or marks down 'E', then he experienced the sensation E. Carney objects to this as follows:

But this will not do, for if whatever he says is E, then it makes no sense to say that he correctly or incorrectly identified E. IF A NECESSARY CONDITION FOR 'E' TO HAVE MEANING IS THAT THE DIARY-KEEPER CAN CORRECTLY (IN CONTRAST WITH INCORRECTLY) IDENTIFY A SENSATION AS E, THEN 'E' HAS NO MEANING.[16]

Here it seems quite clear that it is a necessary condition for something's being a sign in a language that it be possible to use the sign incorrectly. One has, it seems, a fairly clear indication of Mrs. Thomson's second step in a number of passages, among them Mr. Carney's suggestion that in order to take issue with the argument one might attempt to find that which enables the diary-keeper to distinguish between his thinking he is using 'E' correctly and actually using 'E' correctly, an implication being that in any case of a genuine linguistic sign, at least of the type which 'E' purports to be, unwitting misuse must be a possibility. In Carney the analogue to Mrs. Thomson's third step is set out in its most explicit form following Carney's discussion, and rejection, of three possible suggestions as to what might constitute a criterion of correctness in the diary-keeper's situation. Having rejected the suggested criteria, Carney remarks, "If there is no criterion of correctness for 'E', what follows 'E' has no meaning."[17] Here it seems clear that one has a variant of the third step cited by Mrs. Thomson, for the above implies that 'E' has meaning (substituting for "is a kind name in a man's language") only if it is possible to find out whether or not something is an E.

Interestingly enough, one has Carney's explicit statement that no version of a "verification criterion of meaning" is involved in the argument,[18] this being so because all that is required is that there be a way of finding out, on at least SOME occasions, whether or not a sign (his example being the paint chemist's 'C') is being

---

[16] Carney, "Private Language", 562. Emphasis mine.
[17] Carney, "Private Language", 562.
[18] Carney, "Private Language", 561.

used correctly. But this will not serve to separate his 'third step' from the third step which Mrs. Thomson finds, for she notes that unless nothing more than 'logical possibility' is required, then far more will be ruled out than is intended,

... e.g., it would be ruled out that "ace" was a kind-name in English on the ground that I have just destroyed a playing card without looking at it, and it is no longer as a matter of fact possible to find out whether or not it was an ace.[19]

The version presented by Garver can, I think, be made the subject of an exegesis substantially parallelling that which has been suggested for the version set forth by Carney. I will not attempt to sketch this out, since what purports to be the argument is not presented in a manner which lends itself to straightforward interpretation,[20] but in any case it IS clear that the lack of a 'criterion of correctness' is crucial to the conclusion that 'E' cannot function as a sign recording the occurrences of a certain sensation and it seems reasonable to hold that some variant of 'step three' is involved.

Would any or all three accept the contention that they are employing something substantially the same as Mrs. Thomson's third step in their presentations of the argument? This may be doubted, but suppose for a moment that they would do so. If so, then the soundness of the argument hinges on the soundness of some fortunately formulated principle of verifiability. But these formulations have not been presented by the philosophers under consideration in explicit form. (Carney may be held to have come the closest to having done so but then one has his denial that any such principle is being employed, and what is one to make of this?)

If one supposes that Mrs. Thomson's third step would be accepted as a piece of correct interpretation, then it may be worthwhile to note two observations she makes concerning the principle derived from combining the steps of the argument. First, there are two objections to the verifiability principle which can

---

19 Thomson, "Private Languages", 27.
20 See above, p. 25f.

also be made against the new principle. The first objection is a question as to whether the new principle is of any use to us; that is, how is it to be decided whether a putative sign or expression satisfies the principle? Suppose, she suggests, that a man claims to be able to see a color different from all colors which the rest of us claim to be able to see, and that he claims that he can't explain what the color looks like any more than one could explain to a man who is color-blind what redness is. For want of a better word he calls the color 'K'. If one has a question as to whether 'K' IS being used as a kind name, the new principle will, in Mrs. Thomson's estimation, be of little assistance in settling the question:

The principle tells us 'K' is a kind-name in his language only if it is possible to find out whether or not a thing is K. Only if it is possible that WE should find this out, for HIS memory impressions aren't going to count here. Is it possible that we should find out, i.e., come to be able to see which things are K and which are not? One is inclined to say: It is possible only if 'K' IS a kind-name in his language, and not a mere noise. So we come full circle.[21]

The second (and related) objection proposed is the following: Suppose one uses the sign 'C' to stand for the kind of signs in a language which satisfy the principle. One can then ask the question as to whether 'C' satisfies the principle, that is, is it possible to find out whether some particular sign is an instance of C over and above its seeming to some non-sceptic that it does?

... it should be stressed that unless this is possible for some man, then if the new principle is true, 'C' is not a kind-name in anyone's language. In which case, what should we take the principle to be saying?[22]

It is certainly possible that someone will object to Mrs. Thomson's rendering of the argument, but in her defense it might be noted that considerable difficulty has been experienced by many in attempting to obtain a clear view of just what the logical structure

[21] Thomson, "Private Languages", 30.
[22] Thomson, "Private Languages", 31.

of the general argument which is being considered in fact is,[23] and in the absence of clarification on the part of its proponents, it is not an easy matter to determine what would constitute a better interpretation.

In any case, she is surely correct that reliance on some alleged 'logical features' of the concept of a rule is open to serious question, if not untenable, in the formulation of 'step two'. It is, in fact, a rather simple matter to come up with various examples of rules which cannot be violated unwittingly, provided, of course, that a person UNDERSTANDS the rule that he is to follow. As an example of such rules, one might imagine a teacher in a college of veterinary medicine designing a test to determine whether a student has become proficient in detecting the onset of a disease in sheep caused by 'virus X'. Suppose that he presents his student with a group of sheep, each sheep bearing a number, some of which have the slight symptoms which indicate the earliest stage of virus X infection. He might then instruct his student to write down the number of every sheep which, IN HIS JUDGMENT, should be tested for a virus X infection.[24] Given a rule of this type to follow, the student who understands the rule will not be violating the rule unwittingly in writing down the number of a sheep who in actuality does not have any symptoms of virus X infection, as long as it is true that the student BELIEVES (for whatever reason) that particular animal should be tested for virus X. Similarly it seems evident that a rule of the sort which was given to experimental subjects in Dr. Rhine's card-guessing experiments, e.g., to write down the symbol which one thinks, believes or imagines to be the symbol

---

[23] E.g., in commenting on Castaneda's paper, "The Private-Language Argument", V.C. Chappell and James F. Thomson express some question as to just what the 'private-language argument' IS. *Knowledge and Experience: Proceedings of the 1962 Oberlin Colloquium in Philosophy,* C.D. Rollins, ed. (University of Pittsburgh Press), 118 and 124.

[24] A variant of this which would, one supposes, not be of as much value to the teacher but which would be closer to the type of linguistic rule formulated by Mrs. Thomson would be to use, say, 'E' for a kind-name, the kind of thing being 'sheep which in my judgment should be tested for virus X', and to instruct each student to write down an 'E' for each sheep of that kind.

on a card hidden from view would not satisfy Malcolm's second condition on rules.

However, all this shows, is that this second condition on linguistic rules is not an analytic entailment of some kind from the general concept of a rule. Malcolm is certainly at liberty to present some other sort of justification, should he believe that one is needed. Certainly it is true that if a sign is to function as the name of a particular KIND of thing, then it must be logically possible to misuse the sign by applying it to kinds of things other than the kind of thing to which it does have proper application. But this may be simply a basic fact about kind-names rather than something which needs to be justified by an appeal to something else, such as, 'the concept of a rule'.

The questions which are of the greatest interest concern the 'third step' presented by Mrs. Thomson. That something like the third step is needed seems obvious since, supposing the remainder of her reconstruction of the argument to be correct, all one has without it are the stipulations that if 'E' is really the name for a kind of sensation it must be logically possible that a user make an unwitting mistake in applying this term, together with the claim that not only is it the case that (by hypothesis) others cannot find out whether the diary-keeper is using 'E' correctly, but there is nothing which could constitute HIS 'finding out' either, i.e., (1) if 'E' is a kind-name unwitting mistakes must be a possibility, and, (2) NO ONE can find out whether mistakes are in fact being made with 'E'.

A question which is certainly of interest here is: What sort of a justification can be given for step three or perhaps better, are there some general doctrines concerning the nature of language and meaning which contain or constitute an effective equivalent of step three? I believe that there are, but prior to attempting to show that this is so, it will be of considerable interest to examine an argument for the anti-private-language thesis which has not thus far been considered, for in the version of the argument to be considered, some doctrines concerning language and meaning become explicit.

V

THE MANOMETER ARGUMENT

In his paper, "Wittgenstein on Private Language", Newton Garver presents two arguments in addition to the diary-keeper-criterion argument. The first of these additional arguments, is not, so far as I am able to determine, of great weight. Garver writes:

We naturally assume that when you write down 'E' in your diary you must be making a note of something, but Wittgenstein reminds us that the assumption is unjustified [reference to *Investigations* 260]. 'E' is an idle mark; it has no use, no function, no connection with anything. How COULD we make a record of anything with such an idle mark?[1]

What one seems to have here is an argument that a putative sign is a sign in a language only if the sign can be used for a useful purpose. But, in the diary-keeper's situation, writing 'E' serves no useful purpose, and so 'E' cannot be a linguistic sign.

It is not clear that this argument, as stated, has any force, for, supposing one grants the premise, one may ask why it is that, say, keeping a record for one's own amusement is to be ruled out as not sufficiently useful; that is, why is it supposed to be less useful than, say, the record a child might keep of the number of times he sees a peculiar-looking bird dining at the bird-feeding-station he has constructed? Garver notes that Ayer has asked how this activity of the diary-keeper is supposed to be more idle than that of writing down a sign at the same time one observes some 'public' object. Garver's reply is that Wittgenstein would not have

[1] Newton Garver, "Discussion: Wittgenstein on Private Language", *Philosophy and Phenomenological Research*, 20: 394 (1960).

said there was any difference, but that Ayer has missed the point, for the remark in *Investigations* 260 is "on the grammar of making notes, not on the grammar of sensation".[2] In the absence of some explanation as to what the 'grammar of making notes' amounts to, it is difficult to take issue on this point. I suggest that either the above is too weak an objection to deserve much consideration, or else that it has not been made clear enough to allow the opportunity for formulating a reply. In any case the argument noted above has received comparatively little attention by those who have advanced objections to the anti-private-language thesis, either because people have found it to be unclear or have regarded it as being comparatively unimportant.

The other argument or objection, and the discussion which follows it, is considerably more interesting. Garver suggests that we suppose that *"per impossibile"*, a connection between 'E' and a particular sensation were established by means of the private ostensive definition. Suppose that the diary-keeper thereby had a sign 'E' of which he had a private understanding. Garver writes:

> Could we call it the name of a sensation? We would have no justification for doing so, for by calling some mark the name of a sensation we make it intelligible in the common language (or perhaps better: in calling it the name of a sensation we presuppose it to be intelligible in the common language), whereas 'E' is intelligible to you alone [Reference to *Investigations* 261]. Names of sensations have a certain grammar, and 'E' as yet has none.[3]

'E' then cannot be used to keep a record of the alleged sensation, for whatever it is that is supposedly being recorded, 'E' lacks the 'grammar' which would entitle the diary-keeper to call it the name of a sensation.

In some subsequent remarks, Mr. Garver gives an indication of what it is that is required in order to furnish a logical foothold for the required 'grammar'. Garver turns to a discussion of *Investigations* 270, a passage in which one is to imagine that a use is found for the entry in one's diary of the sign 'E', said

---

2   Garver, "Discussion", 394.
3   Garver, "Discussion", 395.

usefulness stemming from one's discovery that upon occurrence of the alleged sensation supposedly being recorded by 'E', a manometer shows that one's blood-pressure rises, the useful result being that henceforth one will be able to tell when one's blood-pressure is rising without recourse to use of the manometer. This fact changes, according to Garver, the entire nature of the situation. First, it becomes possible to give a definition of 'E' as being the sign for the sensation one has when one's blood-pressure rises. From this fact it follows that in writing the sign 'E' in one's diary one is "really making a note of something, *viz* a sensation".[4] In virtue of the manometer correlation, there is no reason to doubt that 'E' really is a sign for a sensation, and, "we have a further justification in calling 'E' the name of a sensation in the fact that 'E' HAS THE GRAMMAR OF A SENSATION WORD: ONLY YOU CAN KNOW WHEN TO WRITE DOWN 'E' AND SO ON."[5]

The second consequence which, according to Mr. Garver, follows from the discovery of the manometer-sensation correlation is that any question as to whether or not the sensations which the diary-keeper is attempting to record by the use of the sign 'E' are REALLY of the same kind or not has COMPLETELY DISAPPEARED, for "If the diary-keeper's blood-pressure has risen, it makes no difference at all whether, in the sense required by the Cartesian, the sensation was 'really' the same or not".[6]

In the consequences drawn from the manometer example, one has an indication of the sort of view of the relationship between sensations and sensation reports which, if true, entails that the putative sign 'E' could not be the name of a sensation. For the moment, I intend to do no more than indicate, in a general way, the type of view which this is in order to set the stage for a discussion of Mr. Garver's claim that once the diary-keeper finds out (by means of the manometer) that his blood-pressure rises whenever he experiences (believes himself to be experiencing?) E, any

4 Garver, "Discussion", 395.
5 Garver, "Discussion", 396.
6 Garver, "Discussion", 396.

question as to whether the sensations were really the same (in Cartesian 'felt quality') disappears.

Toward the beginning of his article, Garver presents an account of how it is that the connections between words and sensations are established in the ordinary language which we all speak and understand. One can come to understand the nature of the connection between names of sensations, such as 'pain', and sensations by attending to the manner in which people learn the meanings of sensation-words. The account given is perhaps excessively familiar to anyone acquainted with the publications of those strongly influenced by 'the later Wittgenstein', but perhaps presentation of what has become tantamount to the standard example in this matter is in order: The child will be taught the verbal expressions of pain in situations in which adults readily see, from his behavior (natural expressions of pain) and his circumstances (e.g., he fell on the sidewalk and skinned his knee) that he is hurt. What is common to all situations providing conditions appropriate for the learning of sensation-words, Garver states, are certain circumstances which always include a particular type of behavior on the part of some living being; the child, or whoever, learns the regular connection between the word, e.g., 'pain', and the relevant circumstances. This entails, according to Mr. Garver, that "the meaning of 'pain' is logically dependent on there being natural expressions of pain", and that, " 'PAIN' DEPENDS UPON PAIN-BEHAVIOR RATHER THAN ON ANY INNER PRIVATE EXPERIENCE FOR ITS MEANING."[7]

It is easy to see that, if the above account is correct, the diary-keeper's project cannot even be described intelligibly, for if the MEANING of 'E' is logically dependent on the existence of publicly observable circumstances and/or behavior naturally associated with 'E' and, if, by hypothesis, there are no such things, then, whatever the diary-keeper might be supposed to be doing with 'E', it would not be true that he was keeping, or attempting to keep, a record of a sensation, for 'E' could not possibly be a sensation-word.

It is perhaps worth noting, in passing, that, supposing that it is

---

[7] Garver, "Discussion", 391. Emphasis mine.

true that the meaning of a sensation-word is logically dependent on there being some natural expression of the sensation and/or other appropriately related publicly observable circumstances, the case of 'pain' constitutes a comparatively favorable example for someone undertaking to spell out what sorts of things constitute typical behavior and circumstances, since, in the case of pain, a great many external causes are easily discriminated, and no one would deny that a great portion of the range of natural pain-behavior is of such a strikingly pronounced nature as to virtually command one's attention. However, it is possible to point to other types of sensations concerning which it is not nearly so obvious how this thesis of Garver's, and of others who hold to substantially the same view, applies. For example, many of us have had the experience which is described as that of "having a ringing in one's ears", this expression referring to or describing a type of auditory experience which is not that of hearing the ringing of a bell, alarm clock or whatever — others will not hear the ringing no matter how closely they listen. Let 'R' be equivalent to the expression "ringing in my ears". The supposition that 'R' is learned on the basis of publicly observable behavior and circumstances is not so plausible as in the case of 'pain'. Some of us who understand the meaning of 'R' would find ourselves hard-pressed at the very least if required to come up with a description of the 'natural expression' of this sensation, or of the circumstances which ordinarily give rise to it.[8] So one may be inclined to suspect that in the case of 'R' one lacks the publicly observable phenomenae which, on the view expressed by Garver, would constitute the prerequisites for teaching the child the meaning of 'R', as well as the necessary precondition for 'R's' having any meaning at all. It is possible that someone subscribing to the view being considered might reply that mastering the use of the sentence, "I hear a ringing in my ears", is in some way 'parasitic' on having learned to say "I hear a bell ringing", in the appropriate circumstances or that one's correct employment

[8] One may learn, e.g., that certain drugs cause one to experience 'R', but knowledge of this sort generally comes subsequent to one's mastery of the expression, "I have a ringing in my ears".

of the former sentence is somehow guaranteed by some sort of a logical or conceptual 'connection in the language itself'. However, in the absence of a clearer explanation of what the suggested explanations amount to it is not obvious that a plausible account is available. One seems to be left with the question as to how, if the account given by Garver and others of the necessary pre-requisites for the teaching of sensation-words is a correct model, it would be possible for one to know, or have sufficiently good reason to believe, that one's child was not (PER MALCOLM) misusing the expression "ringing in my ears" to report a mental picture of a bell or a feeling of light-headedness or whatever. If it is true that there are no natural behavioral indicators for the type of experience reported by 'R' and no customary sets of circumstances, other than linguistic avowals, on the basis of which, in the ordinary course of existence,[9] one has warrant for attributing 'R' to others, then it seems that there is at least a *prima facie* difficulty in pre-senting an account of the way in which 'R' is learned which would be, in its essentials, congruent with the account given for 'pain', and similarly in showing how it is that this linguistic expression has meaning.

However, it may be that it can be shown that this putative counter-example constitutes no real difficulty for the account sketched out by Garver. In any case I believe that there is a more interesting avenue of objection to the claim that the meaning of a sensation-word is logically dependent on there being some natural expression of the sensation and/or appropriately related observable circumstances.

I want to turn to a consequence of this doctrine of logical dependency indicated by Garver in his discussion of the mano-meter example. Once the diary-keeper finds (via the manometer) that his blood-pressure rises whenever he experiences the putative sensation or whatnot in question, then whatever this UNDING may have been said to be beforehand, it becomes a *bona fide* sensation in virtue of the 'outward criterion' furnished by the phenomenon

---

[9] I.e., excluding the case in which a physician might infer that his patient is experiencing 'R' on the basis that the patient is taking a particular drug.

of rising blood-pressure indicated by the manometer. The logical dependency of the meaning of 'E' on this publicly accessible phenomenon is, according to Garver, a TOTAL dependency such that it follows that the problem of its identity has completely disappeared; the questions as to whether these sensations which cause or indicate a rise in blood-pressure are, "in the Cartesian sense", the same or not is one which "makes no difference at all".[10]

What Garver is saying here, one must suppose, is not simply that the question as to whether the sensation is the same or not, apart from external indicators, is of no PRACTICAL importance, but rather that the question is, in virtue of the logical dependence existing between outward criteria and the meaning of sensation-words, at bottom unintelligible.

Malcolm, in his discussion of this alleged logical dependency clearly indicates that the connection between outward criteria, i.e., behavior and material circumstances, and the meanings of sensation-words is of such a nature that the intelligibility of supposing that a sensation might change so as to be other than that indicated by outward criteria is to be conceptually ruled out. For example, in response to a proposal that there are not less than TWO essential features of sensation words, namely that they (1) refer to our sensations and (2) contain allusions either to behavior or to material facts associated with these sensations, Malcolm objects as follows:

But if my words WITHOUT THOSE allusions can refer to my sensations, then what is alluded to is only CONTINGENTLY related to the sensations. Adding the allusions to what can be seen and touched, [Reference to Peter Strawson's "Critical Notice: *Philosophical Investigations*", p. 86.] will not help one bit in making us understand one another. For the behavior that is for me contingently associated with 'the sensation of pain' may be for you, contingently associated with 'the sensation of tickling' ... my 'sensation of red' may be your 'sensation of blue' ....[11]

---

[10] Garver, "Discussion", 396.
[11] Norman Malcolm, "Wittgenstein's *Philosophical Investigations*", *The Philosophy of Mind*, V.C. Chappell, ed. (Englewood Cliffs, N.J., Prentice-Hall, 1962), 96.

In his article on the private-language-question, Carney makes a similar assertion. A view of the language-sensation relationship which holds that the meanings of sensation words are in some sense ultimately derived from sensations themselves (the view which makes the diary-keeper project seem intelligible) is not a correct view, according to Carney; if such WERE a correct view of the nature of language, it would be possible that various people might have qualitatively different color-experiences when they report seeing red. Such a picture of language, Carney states,

> ... makes it necessary to assume that people have 'qualitatively similar' sensations in order to explain how communication is possible .... Now if the argument presented is correct, this assumption ... is neither true nor false. In order for it to be true or false, it must be possible for there to be sensations from which words derive their meanings. But there cannot be such sensations, because words cannot derive their meanings from sensations. The assumption does function to make experience intelligible, but experience, we might say, needs to be made intelligible only because the picture of language makes it appear unintelligible.[12]

Suppose we consider, one of the specific consequences of what one might call the 'outward-criterion-meaning relationship' indicated in the above-quoted remark. The 'inverted-spectrum hypothesis' is ruled out on logical grounds. That is, a hypothesis which occurred to some of us quite early in life that, e.g., it might be the case that when brother John looks at the clear sky he has an experience of color which I, if I were (*per impossibile*) to have the same color-experience, would call "seeing a reddish color", really is not an intelligible supposition at all.

One may be inclined to object at this point that to hold that the inverted-spectrum hypothesis is a logically incoherent notion is to advance a claim which runs counter to an implicit conceptual scheme which it seems reasonable to suspect, in the absence of evidence to the contrary, all reasonably intelligent native speakers of the language have (for one might suppose that a sample survey of competent native speakers would show that the hypothesis

[12] James D. Carney, "Private Language: The Logic of Wittgenstein's Argument", *Mind*, 69: 564 (1960).

would not be considered LOGICALLY odd), and that this in itself counts as a consideration against it. If one finds merit in Peirce's argument for a warranted presumption in favor of the adequacy of human (and animal) intelligence in coming to an understanding of the basic features of the world, then one may regard such an objection as having considerable weight. In any case, that this implied conclusion that the inverted-spectrum hypothesis does not describe a logically possible state-of-affairs DOES (if it does) run counter to what one might call one's 'native (non-academic) intuitions' in the matter is not, in itself, something to be said in favor of the argument or doctrine which implies it. For although it may be a mark of genius to be able to advance a theory which has at least the appearance of being supported by sound and coherent argument, and which nevertheless leads to conclusions which run counter to our common understanding of some basic feature of existence, the counter-intuitive character of the conclusion entailed is not a feature which IN ITSELF serves to recommend the considerations advanced in its support.

In the chapter which follows, an attempt will be made to explore the question as to whether or not there is anything which might (this is to be a logical 'might') happen which would give us some rational warrant for supposing that a simplified variant of the inverted-spectrum hypothesis had actually been instantiated. In attempting to construct such a case, it will be of interest to attempt to determine whether (A) what one may rather imprecisely call 'logical-linguistic' considerations would be the only relevant considerations in determining whether or not a claim that the inverted-spectrum hypothesis has been instantiated, or whether (B) certain empirical facts would be relevant in deciding whether or not the inverted-spectrum hypothesis, or some variant of it, had actually been instantiated.

It may be worthwhile to pause for a moment at this point to indicate more clearly what is being attempted in the discussion of the inverted-spectrum hypothesis which follows, and what logical relation the inverted-spectrum hypothesis has to the anti-private-language thesis.

The relationship is as follows: If the 'outward criteria-sensation-word-meaning' relationship advocated by Garver, Malcolm and Carney is a correct account, then it follows, not only that the hypothetical diary-keeper cannot be keeping any record of a sensation with his use of the putative sign 'E', but also that the propositions comprising P in Chapter One are false. The truth of the account in question would also entail the consequence that the inverted-spectrum hypothesis, or any simplified variant (such as the transposition of TWO primary colors in one's visual experience) is conceptually unintelligible.

Therefore, a possible avenue of attack on the sensation-word-meaning account advocated by Garver, Malcolm and Carney is that of attempting to show that the inverted-spectrum hypothesis (or some simplified variant) IS intelligible. If it can be shown that the inverted-spectrum hypothesis is intelligible, then it follows that the account of the sensation-word-meaning relationship presented by Garver, Malcolm and Carney is incorrect. I shall attempt to show that the inverted-spectrum hypothesis is intelligible (that is, that no hidden absurdities are contained therein) by arguing that there could be sound empirical evidence indicating the actual existence of a simplified version of the inverted spectrum in a particular person's visual experience. This is not to imply that the possibility of empirical evidence is a necessary condition for the meaningfulness of a hypothesis of the above sort; rather, I am inclined to believe that it is not. However, the possibility of the existence of sound empirical evidence for the truth of a particular proposition is certainly a sufficient condition for meaningfulness, and I believe it possible to show that there could be sound empirical evidence indicating the existence of such a state-of-affairs.

VI

THE INVERTED-SPECTRUM HYPOTHESIS AND THE QUESTION OF EVIDENCE

I will now attempt to construct an example of the sort of case which would at least appear to give some rational ground, for those not convinced that the outward-criterion doctrine is correct, for suspecting that an instance of transposed color-experience has been found: Suppose that a man, call him Mr. B, becomes afflicted with an illness which baffles his physician, such that this physician finds himself forced, by the peculiar syndrome of symptoms manifested, to conclude that the illness is due to a new mutant strain of virus. As the illness becomes more severe, Mr. B gradually loses his sight until, at the time when the syndrome reaches its most acute stage he becomes totally blind. Happily, however, as the disease abates, he gradually recovers his sight. Yet, in at least one respect it appears that Mr. B's vision has not returned to normal, for he consistently mistakes red for blue and *vice versa*. He confides to a friend that his nurse Polly, a comely lass, looks strangely unappealing to him, for her eyes look red and her lips (as he sees them) are blue; the sky is not so attractive either. It looked much better prior to his illness—pale red is just not an appropriate color. Now if Mr. B continues to assert, with sincerity, that his color-experiences of red and blue have been reversed, apparently through some effect of his illness, then one has the sort of case in which some of us would suspect that an instance of transposed color-experience has occurred.

One type of explanation for Mr. B's sincere claim would be the explanation that Mr. B's memory is faulty in a peculiar respect, that although he BELIEVES that his perceptions of red and blue have been reversed, the belief is simply mistaken. Justification for the claim that Mr. B's circumstances must be explained as a case of defective memory could in turn be either an argument based on philosophical account of the sensation-word-meaning relationship (e.g., the outward-criterion doctrine) or on empirical grounds, i.e., on the basis of certain empirical facts deemed relevant to resolution of the question.

Suppose one considers the two forms of the defective-memory explanation. It seems evident that the only type of explanation available to a proponent of the outward-criterion doctrine would be one essentially like the following: The meaning of color-words is in no way dependent on any sort of 'private experience' of color; rather the meaning of these words is altogether logically dependent on external (or 'public') states-of-affairs in the same way that the meaning of 'pain' is thus dependent. It follows that any hypothesis that Mr. B is really seeing something different is something which, despite its surface appearance of intelligibility, is at bottom absurd, and absurd because unintelligible. The only intelligible explanation of Mr. B's situation is that, due, one supposes, to the effects of his strange illness, he has forgotten the correct use of two color-words, misremembering the use of the two words 'red' and 'blue' (together with 'reddish' etc.). As for his claim that prior to his illness these colors actually looked different to him, this claim, supposing it to be sincere, can only be regarded as a queer memory phenomenon.

The above would be, in substance, the sort of explanation compatible with the outward-criterion doctrine. In shortened form, it is that it follows from logical grounds (the meaning-criterion relation) alone that the only possible explanation for Mr. B's sincere claim is that of a defective memory with respect to these matters.

Let us now note briefly the characteristics of the alternate form of the defective-memory explanation. This hypothesis states that Mr. B's sincere claims MAY stem from a memory which has become defective in the relevant respects, but, unlike the first form, holds that this possibility is one for which there could conceivably be empirical evidence tending either to confirm or eliminate it. The considerations which would support it are not of a 'logical-linguistic' or 'logical-conceptual' nature (that is, no variant of the outward-criterion doctrine is regarded as constituting support), but rather it is a hypothesis whose denial is intelligible, to which empirical evidence, whether in fact obtainable or not, would be relevant.

The second TYPE of explanation of what has happened in the case of Mr. B is simply that what he claims to be the case is both intelligible and true, that is, an instantiation of transposed color-experience has occurred; where he formerly saw red, he now sees what he, prior to his illness, called 'blue' and *vice versa*. The second form of the defective-memory theory, though intelligible, is not a correct account of what has happened and there may be evidence to show this. The first form of defective-memory explanation is not correct, since it denies the intelligibility of Mr. B's claim, and the claim which it denies IS intelligible.

Suppose that we desire to determine, rationally that is, which explanation is true. We could examine these putative possibilities in the order in which they have been presented, starting with the first form of the defective-memory explanation, which is a consequence of the outward-criterion doctrine, the first general question being whether the outward-criterion doctrine furnishes a correct account of the sensation-word-meaning relationship; one would review the considerations which have been advanced in support of this doctrine hoping to evaluate the strength of the arguments supporting it. However, there is reason to doubt that this would be the most effective strategy in settling the question, for, if one could show the possibility of certain sorts of empirical evidence having a bearing on the question of rational selection of an explanation, then the first form of the defective-memory theory is ruled out, being a consequence of the outward-criterion doctrine which holds that only certain LOGICAL-CONCEPTUAL considerations are relevant.

Let us assume, for the moment at least, that the two alternatives to the first form of the defective-memory explanation are not unintelligible. What sorts of evidence would appear to have a bearing on coming to a reasoned decision as to which of these accounts purporting to describe B's situation is the correct one?

Two sorts of approaches suggest themselves. One of these would be that of adding to our fund of knowledge concerning Mr. B by determining whether the transposition is restricted to cases in which the colors viewed are simply roughly standard exemplifications of red or blue, or whether it carries over to instances of mixed pigments such that, if we mix red and yellow pigments and obtain an orange mixture, he identifies the resulting color as 'green' (which would be the result of mixing blue and yellow pigments), or whether it does not carry over in the way in which one might expect if there were actually a change in a subject's experience of colors. On the other hand, if this misidentification did not carry over, one would be inclined to regard a memory-failure explanation as having considerably more plausibility, for in view of the lack of 'carryover' to pigment MIXTURES, no strain would be put on the failure of memory explanation, whereas its alternative, that B's color-experiences HAVE changed, to be coherent, would have to be amended to include some sort of explanation as to why, if red pigment (under normal conditions of illumination) does give Mr. B the experience of 'seeing blue', red pigment mixed with yellow pigment does not (under normal lighting and other conditions of observation which could be specified) give him the experience of seeing an apparently green patch rather than the orange patch which others see.

If there were this systematic carryover into all cases of colors produced by mixed pigments having red or blue or both as components, then many would be inclined to hold that this systematic carryover furnished a strong warrant for concluding that, singular though the case may be, Mr. B's experience of colors has changed in a remarkable manner. It should perhaps be emphasized that the question, supposing it to be a question, is not conclusively decided beyond the shadow of a possible objection, one way or the other, by the occurrence or non-occurrence of a carryover of systematically deviant color-reports into cases of mixed pigments, but if deviant color-reports do carry over, the complexity of a memory-failure hypothesis must be increased, whereas, if they do not, an elaboration of the relatively simple change-in-experience hypothesis is in order. Supposing there is something rational in the tendency to prefer a simple hypothesis which is able to remain simple in accounting for new facts to a hypothesis roughly equal in original simplicity, which must be revised in the direction of complexity as additional facts relating to that which it purports to explain come to light, the presence or absence of carryover in B's color-reports should incline one toward acceptance of one sort of explanation being considered in preference to the other.

The second possible avenue of approach I want to suggest is that of finding out something about certain features of Mr. B's brain, eyes, and perhaps the optic nerves.

It has been established that when pain is induced in a human being, instruments designed to record "brain-waves" record a characteristic 'spike' pattern. Suppose that psychologist or physiologists who do this sort of research find that there also are characteristic patterns of brain-waves in all tested cases of color-perception. In the course of determining that this is so, they have constructed a 'blue room' and a 'red room' and so on, enclosures whose interiors are painted blue, red, orange and so on respectively. Research personnel have found that when experimental subjects are placed in the red room under suitable conditions, characteristic patterns, which experimenters call 'R-Waves' show up on the recording instrument, in the blue room a characteristic pattern called 'B-Waves' is recorded, and so on. So, let's present (with his willing cooperation) Mr. B to the persons engaged in this type of research, explain our question to them, and ask them to subject him to tests. Suppose that upon completion of the tests we are informed that something unparalleled has occurred: When Mr. B was in the blue room, the instruments recorded 'R-Waves', when placed in the red room, 'B-Waves' were recorded, on to the orange room and there 'G-Waves' were manifested, and so on. Some of us would regard results of this sort as corroboration of Mr. B's claim that where we see red he really does have the experience of seeing blue. It is perhaps well to mention here that there are objections to any claim that test results of the above sort would really constitute evidence for transposed color-experience, and in time I wish to bring these out together with some considerations concerning their strength, but in order to come to an evaluation of such objections, it will be a useful propaedeutic to consider other methods of obtaining evidence concerning the truth of Mr. B's claim which suggest themselves.

We are free to imagine that the research personnel we have consulted suggest a further test: Send Mr. B on to the people who understand the mode of operation of the retinal receptors. Mr. B agrees to submit to such an examination. The retina specialists find factor 'X' which is known to be essential to perception of red and blue to be absent, and 'in its place' a factor (substance, functional pattern or whatever) hitherto unencountered is discovered, which the experimenters have decided to call factor 'Y'. Once again it at least SEEMS that we have another bit of confirmation for Mr. B's claim.

Still leaving the question open as to whether the test results which have been imagined would really qualify as contributing to confirmation or disconfirmation of Mr. B's claim that his color-experiences are transposed, what sort of tests might be imagined which, on the same general view of confirming evidence, would appear to provide some confirmation for a defective-memory hypothesis of the kind holding that empirical considerations are relevant to its truth or falsity. It has already been noted that a lack of 'carryover' to mixed pigments would seem, on the surface of things at least, to provide some rational basis for preferring a defective-memory explanation. Parenthetically it might be added that if it were the case that certain other systematic mistakes were to show up, for instance with 'cat' and 'dog' and 'table' and 'chair', one would be inclined to regard this phenomenon as indicating that something rather serious had happened to his memory of the use of words, but if one extends this sort of thing very far, Mr. B loses the appearance of being a rational being at all, and I think it is essential, if the question of the intelligibility of the inverted-spectrum hypothesis is to lend itself to a discussion of possible evidence, that the Mr. B in our example be, by hypothesis, a substantially rational being. Therefore, I do not believe it would be helpful to the present discussion to pursue a suggestion of evidence of this sort very far. So to go back to the question as to whether any supposed evidence of the type yielded in the brain-wave or retinal examination examples could be found which would indicate that defective memory is the rationally preferable explanation, it seems that it is not especially difficult to construct an analogue. One must presuppose, as in the other examples, a rather high degree of sophistication in techniques for gaining information about the nervous system, but this is, I submit, allowable in the absence of some evidence of logical impossibility.

Suppose that the brain-wave recorders have located a center (or centers) in the brain whose normal functioning is supposed, from evidence which has been gathered, to be essential to correct memory of words of a certain type, be they color-words, "kind-names" or whatever will serve the purpose. We are free to refine this further to the point of imagining that a certain typical brain-wave is manifested by this area when persons are engaged in speech involving the employment of color-words, and that these waves have been named 'C-Waves'. One can go a step further and suppose that variant patterns of C-Waves have been discerned and that one of these, call it 'C_1' has invariably occurred when experimental subjects have given descriptions employing the word 'red'. We hand Mr. B over to these people and tell them what our question is and request that relevant tests be performed. Upon completion of the tests, the supervisor of this operation reports that Mr. B is indeed an unusual case in that when describing color pattern as being red and white, brain wave C_2 is manifested instead of the normal C_1, and that a similar transposition occurs when he describes a pattern as blue and white namely C_1, which normally occurs as a correlate of a subject's employment of the word 'red', is in evidence instead of C_2. If results of the above sort were obtained, we would, it is being argued, have evidence that Mr. B's color-word memory center is abnormal, this in turn counting as evidence for the truth of the defective-memory theory.

If considerations of the above sort would in fact qualify as evidence for and against a claim of the sort made by our hypothetical Mr. B, then there is something suspicious about the elimination of the inverted-spectrum hypothesis on *a priori* grounds. One has reason to suppose that if the truth of the outward-criterion doctrine eliminates the logical possibility of the inverted-spectrum hypothesis, the outward-criterion doctrine is simply not true.

Having carried this hypothetical case of Mr. B this far, it is worth pausing to consider the sorts of evidence or considerations which may have cohered in such a way as to justify (on a view of the nature of justification which I have not yet made explicit) at least a presumption in favor of the truth of his claim. We will suppose that the following statements are true:

(1) Mr. B sincerely claims that his perceptual experience of red and blue colors has been reversed.

(2) Mr. B professes to understand the claims that his memory for certain color-words has become defective, and objects to these accounts as being manifestly untrue. He claims that if WE were in his situation, we too would KNOW that defective memory is not a correct explanation.

(3) Mr. B's misidentification of red and blue carries over into the case of mixed pigments in a systematic way, e.g., a red and yellow pigment mixture is identified as 'green', a blue and yellow mixture as 'orange', and so on.

(4) Records of brain-wave patterns produced by Mr. B when run through the red room, blue room, green room, orange room test series show a systematic transposition of brain wave patterns, i.e., 'R-Waves' and only 'R-Waves' (in the class of 'color-perception-waves') are manifested in the blue room, 'B-Waves' in the red room, and so on.

(5) Examination of Mr. B's retinas shows that factor 'X' is absent, having been replaced by a heretofore unencountered factor, which the retinal examiners have baptized as factor 'Y'.

(6) Brain-waves emitted from what research has indicated to be 'color-word memory center(s)' show a normal pattern, the normal 'C_1' being manifested as Mr. B employs the word 'red' in a description, and so on.

The first two statements are tied into the hypothetical situation of Mr. B as initially formulated, their truth being held to be sufficient to raise a question as to whether Mr. B's claim is true. The truth of (3) supports Mr. B's claim in at least one respect, namely that a revision of the defective-memory hypothesis in the direction of complexity is required if the defective-memory hypothesis is to account for the fact stated in (3), whereas no revision is required in the case of the explanation which holds that the relevant color-experiences have actually been transposed. The truth of (4) and (5) furnishes reasons for preferring to believe that Mr. B's claim is correct in a direct manner, in that they declare certain states-of-affairs to exist which we, on the perhaps partially implicit basis of a conceptual scheme concerning the relation of physiology to perceptual experience, would suppose to be correlated to alterations in perceptual experience. The truth of (6) can be regarded as an indirect confirmation of color-experience transposition (supposing that defective memory is the only other explanation which we regard as relevant) since, on the basis of what is believed to be true concerning a connection between certain physical processes and memory, we have obtained no evidence that an alteration of the supposedly relevant physiological factors has taken place. Statement (6) indicates an absence of empirical support for the competing defective-memory explanation.

A number of objections might be made to the above account. The first objection or question which may be envisaged might run somewhat as follows: "Of course the truth of statements one through six would furnish at least presumptive grounds for preferring the color-transposition hypothesis as an explanation of Mr. B's circumstances, and granted one could imagine test results which would tend to confirm the defective-memory explanation, that is, suppose we find, contrary to statements three through six, no 'carry-over', no atypical wave patterns in the red, blue, green and orange room tests, nor any discernible retinal changes (though our techniques in such examinations lack nothing in refinement), and suppose the color-word memory centers do manifest atypical waves in a systematic way, such results would equally incline a rational man to prefer defective memory as the correct account of what (contrary to Mr. B's impressions in this matter) has actually happened. However, suppose some of what we take to be evidence inclines us (on the general presuppositions indicated) toward accepting a transposition hypothesis while other factors incline us to accept defective memory — what if there is a conflict of evidence? — wouldn't this show that the presuppositions in virtue of which we are inclined to regard the truth of statements three through six as evidence for a transposition hypothesis are really not well-founded, and perhaps complete misconceptions?"

The appropriate reply is, it would seem, the open admission that test results of a sufficiently conflicting character would constitute grounds for reconsideration and revision or elimination of some or all of the elements of our initial conceptual scheme. Whether or not such a revision WOULD be undertaken in the face of apparently incompatible results (supposing we have NO grounds for supposing errors in test procedure) is another question, for though rationality might indicate the need for such revision, there are, it has been argued, in the scientific community of the real world we actually live in, certain psychological and sociological factors operating which, in particular sorts of situations (e.g., when a body of theory and/or preconceptions which have, in the past been regarded as adequate appears to be threatened), have been responsible for an opposition to incompatible data and theories which could not be justified on rational grounds.[1] But the above observations are carrying us rather far afield; to sum up, it IS conceivable that the test results might be incompatible with our psychological theories. If such proved to be the case, then these theories would need some looking into if it could be shown that the reason for the apparent conflict did not lie in inaccurate results due to faulty investigative techniques.

However, if the results in the hypothetical case under consideration were *not* conflicting, then we would have reasons for preferring the transposition hypothesis to the defective-memory hypothesis (or *vice versa*), and this is what, for the sake of the argument, is being supposed. If all test results are of the kind which (on the basis of our psychological theories) support the

---

[1] E.g., Alfred DeGrazia, "The Scientific Reception System", *The American Behavioral Scientist,* 7: 38-55 (1963). The entire issue is devoted to matters relevant to this topic.

transposition hypothesis, then we not only have, it is being argued, reason to believe that the transposition hypothesis is true, but further, we have some additional reason (in that these theories have NOT given rise to incompatible evidence), for regarding our initial psychological theories, presuppositions or whatever, as sound.

Supposing that all test results indicated the plausibility of the transposition hypothesis, what effect would knowledge of these results have on a rational man who regards the transposition hypothesis as intelligible, but had initially been inclined to prefer a defective-memory explanation? The answer, I think, is fairly simple. Since the initial explanation preferred by him would be the defective-memory account which holds that empirical evidence would be relevant, the fact that no evidence for it was yielded by test results, whereas evidence for color-experience transposition had been manifested, would cause him (assuming he shared roughly the same conception of WHAT would be relevant) to abandon his explanation in favor of the transposition hypothesis.

A more interesting question is whether the test results regarded as indicating the truth of the transposition hypothesis would constitute a refutation of the first form of the defective-memory explanation, i.e., the form which holds that the question is decideable on logical-conceptual grounds, and consequently of the outward-criterion doctrine itself. It has been noted by more than one contemporary philosopher that 'proofs' and 'refutations' in any strict sense of these words, are hard (if not impossible) to come by in philosophy. That this is so is not the sort of claim to which some of us would raise an objection. There is reason to suppose that a proponent of the outward-criterion doctrine, and its consequent, the first form of the defective-memory explanation, would not regard the hypothetical evidence cited in this chapter as constituting evidence for the transposition hypothesis. In the chapter which follows I propose to examine some objections which may be anticipated to any claim that such test results would really qualify as evidence.

VII

AN EXAMINATION OF SOME OBJECTIONS

Let us consider the sorts of objections one might anticipate, from someone holding that the outward-criterion doctrine is true, to a claim that there is, in the case of Mr. B, evidence that certain color-experiences have been transposed. First, it must be acknowledged that what will be presented here must be to some degree speculative, yet I believe the general line of argument is indicated in the writings of a number of persons who have been considerably influenced by Wittgenstein, perhaps most clearly in certain arguments appearing in Malcolm's monograph, *Dreaming*.[1] Also, it must be acknowledged that the sorts of possible objections which will be indicated, would be more skilfully presented by someone holding to the truth of the outward-criterion doctrine. Last, it is not suggested that the objections which will be noted should be attributed to Wittgenstein; no exegesis of Wittgenstein's writings is being attempted.

Taking one's clues from Malcolm's monograph, it seems reasonable to suppose that objections of the following sort would be made:

(1) Justification for the ascription of psychological predicates must ultimately rest on the existence of criteria warranting such ascriptions; there are criteria which warrant ascription of the expression "understands the word 'red'" and Mr. B's behavior does not satisfy these criteria.

(2) Construing the test results as evidence for the transposition hypo-

---

[1] Norman Malcolm, *Dreaming* (*Studies in Philosophical Psychology*, R.F. Holland,ed.) (London, Routledge and Kegan-Paul, 1959).

thesis involves a change of meaning of crucial expressions such as "understands the meaning of the word 'red'", and "sees a red color".

As partial justification for supposing that something essentially similar to (1) would be advanced, the following statement by Malcolm indicates the sorts of considerations which would give rise to something of this sort. In *Dreaming*, Malcolm writes:

... one may be inclined to think that there cannot be a CRITERION (something that settles a question with certainty) of someone's having a sore foot or having dreamt, but merely various 'outer' phenomena that are empirically correlated with sore feet and dreams. This view, however, is self-contradictory: WITHOUT CRITERIA FOR THE OCCURRENCE OF THESE THINGS THE CORRELATIONS COULD NOT BE ESTABLISHED. Without criteria the sentences 'His foot is sore', 'He had a dream', would have no use, either correct or incorrect.[2]

On this view, justification for ascription of psychological predicates must ultimately rest on the existence of characteristic behavior and circumstances on the basis of which such ascriptions are, under normal circumstances, warranted on grounds OTHER than that of being contingently correlated to what it is that is being ascribed, the relation to the relevant ascribed phenomenon being in some sense a conceptual one rather than that of being contingently-connected evidence. The nature of the criterial relation is somewhat difficult to make clear, but perhaps the following illustration may serve as an example indicating the sort of point Malcolm has in mind: Seeing Mr. B taking aspirin MAY furnish a warrant for holding that Mr. B is in pain, this being so in virtue of a known correlation between being in pain and the taking of aspirin; however, we know of this correlation only because there exist typical pain-producing circumstances and pain-behavior on the basis of which we have learned to ascribe pain to others, and the relation of these circumstances and the characteristic behavior CANNOT be of the contingent 'aspirin-pain' variety, for there is nothing further to which the typical circumstances and behavior could be correlated, that is, there is not another, INDEPENDENTLY IDENTIFIABLE something called 'B's pain' to which an observer might correlate pain-

---

[2] Malcolm, *Dreaming,* 60f. Emphasis is mine.

producing circumstances and pain-behavior; the behavior and circumstances themselves furnish the warrant — they constitute a 'criterion':

... that so-and-so is the criterion of Y is a matter, not of experience, but 'definition' [reference to *Investigations* 354]. The satisfaction of the criterion of Y ... repeats the kind of case in which we were taught to say 'Y'.[3]

If one accepts this account requiring the existence of criteria justifying the ascription of mental predicates, an account which has a great deal of initial plausibility, an argument can be constructed to show that Mr. B does not understand (has forgotten or systematically misunderstands) the meanings or uses of certain color words, for on the basis of the account of justification indicated above, it follows that expressions involving the word 'understanding' have meaning (or a correct use) only if there are criteria for correct application of these linguistic expressions. If this is so, it can be shown that Mr. B does not understand the words 'red', 'blue', and so on:

First, supposing that there exist criteria which would justify an ascription of color-blindness, it is plain that Mr. B's behavior (taking 'behavior' to include verbal behavior) would NOT justify such an ascription since, by hypothesis, he is able to distinguish a blue patch from a red patch and so on into the case of pigment mixtures, and his 'mistakes' with respect to these colors are consistent, rather than the type of unsystematic mistakes and manifest guessing which one would suppose to be exhibited in the case of color-blindness.

Supposing that there are criteria constituting the only ultimate justification for attributing an understanding of the color-words in question, it seems evident that Mr. B's relevant verbal behavior fails to indicate that he understands these words, this being so because (supposing that the 'criterial behavior' required would consist of, or include as an essential element, facility in identifying

---

[3] Norman Malcolm, "Wittgenstein's *Philosophical Investigations*", *The Philosophy of Mind,* V.C. Chappell, ed. (Englewood Cliffs, N.J., Prentice-Hall, 1962), 87.

red objects as 'red', blue objects as 'blue', and so on) Mr. B neither manifests the relevant criterial behavior nor any known empirical correlate. Consequently, it follows that Mr. B does not understand the meaning (or 'use') of these words.

It is altogether too easy to oversimplify, and thereby misrepresent the philosophical view which one is attempting to criticize, and it may be that the above does not constitute a fair account of the sort of objection which would be raised with respect to the transposition hypothesis and Mr. B. Possibly the objection would not be this simple in form, for perhaps it could be held, without being inconsistent with the criterion account, that one might grant on the basis of some subordinate criterion, such as, say, Mr. B's ability to describe scenes of his childhood correctly with respect to colors, that he does have a partial or limited understanding of the relevant color words, and it may be that other similar qualifications might be made. However, no refinement of the indicated sort would allow a proponent of the outward-criterion doctrine to concede the possibility that our hypothetical man has a correct understanding of the word 'red' in the sort of situation in which, pointing to an object which the rest of us see as blue in color, he declares that what HE sees is a red color patch, elephant or whatever; the possibility that his account is a true account must be denied in order to be consistent with the outward-criterion doctrine and the criterion account of justification,[4] for, supposing that there necessarily exists a criterion which, by convention or conceptual connection, warrants one in ascribing a full understanding of a color-word to someone who is neither blind nor color-blind, proficiency in correct identification of examples to which the word applies has the appearance of being the strongest available candidate, and Mr. B's behavior would fail to satisfy such a criterion.

---

[4] From this point on it will be essential to bear in mind the distinction between the claim that the MEANINGS of sensation-words are totally dependent on publicly-observable criteria, which I refer to as the outward-criterion doctrine, and the criterion account of justification, i.e., the claim that the possibility of one's being JUSTIFIED IN ASCRIBING A SENSATION TO SOMEONE ELSE is dependent upon there being a logical or conceptual connection between observable behavior and circumstances and the sensation or mental whatnot being ascribed.

A concession that 'in some sense' Mr. B understands the relevant color words will in no way close the essential gap between the defective-memory theory derived from the outward-criterion doctrine and the transposition hypothesis, for the sense in which an understanding might be acknowledged would not affect the contention that Mr. B's sincere claim that the red patch (under normal conditions of observation) looks blue to him involves a (queer) misunderstanding of the relevant color-words.

Of course Mr. B, in the interest of practical every-day communication, could in time acquire new habits in the employment of the relevant color-words which would bring his speech into conformity with general use of these terms, and in so doing, he would then satisfy what we have supposed to be the basic or fundamental criterion for the understanding of these color-words. But the account which would follow from the criterion approach to this matter. namely that he has REGAINED (a complete?) understanding of these color-words presents one with a counter-intuitive account of what has happened, and certainly one which Mr. B would not accept. However, whether or not Mr. B would be satisfied with the 'regained understanding' explanation, it is nevertheless true that such an account is the only acceptable type of explanation available provided that the outward-criterion doctrine is correct and that the 'regained understanding' explanation is the only type of explanation compatible with it.

The question then, is whether the criterion account concerning justification of ascriptions of psychological predicates is true, or possibly better (since perhaps more easily decidable), whether it is the only plausible account available to us. Prior to exploring this question, it may be in order to sketch out the second anticipated avenue of objection,[5] since a special feature of at least some versions of the criterion account (e.g., Malcolm's) is involved in it.

One of the topics taken up in the course of Malcolm's monograph, *Dreaming*, is the claim by certain research psychologists, that a method has been found, by means of correlating brain-wave

[5]   Above, p. 78f.

phenomenae and observable behavioral factors (such as episodes of rapid eye-movements while asleep) with the dream-reports of experimental subjects, of measuring the actual time span taken up by the dreams of those experimental subjects. Malcolm objects to this claim on the ground that the scientists who have made this claim have unwittingly altered our ordinary concept of 'dream' and hence are using the word 'dream' in an extraordinary and misleading way.

Malcolm's argument that this is so runs, in somewhat simplified form, as follows:[6] Warrant for ascribing dreams to others must ultimately rest on the existence of a criterion which justifies such ascriptions. This criterion, Malcolm argues, must be the other's (sincere) dream report or description of his dream. A criterion is conceptually related to what is ascribed (or the concept involved, which in this case is 'dream') in such a way as to place certain restrictions on the conceptual character of what it is that is being ascribed. For example, the ordinary dream report furnishes one with no means of determining a precise span of 'clock time' in which the reported dream may be said to have actually occurred. From this it follows, according to Malcolm, that our ordinary concept "dream" is not one of a something having the kind of duration which could be measured by real[7] clocks. What the experimenters have done, according to Malcolm, is to introduce a NEW criterion (brain-waves and rapid eye-movements), this introduction having the conceptual consequence of altering what is meant by 'dream' in such fashion that claim that dreams can be measured does NOT have application to dreams in the ordinary sense of the word.

If Malcolm's objection is sound, it is fairly easy to see that analogous objections can be constructed which would show the emptiness of any claim that evidence has been found for an instantiation of the inverted spectrum, for suppose that one holding to Malcolm's views in this matter states that the (or the PRIMARY)

---

[6] Malcolm, *Dreaming*, Chapter XIII.

[7] Clocks which are physical objects as distinguished from a clock one might dream about.

criterion for ascribing an understanding of a color-word to a person is that the person in question must be able to pick out the color designated by the word. It is true that Mr. B could do this by calling what appears to him to be red, 'blue' and so on, but suppose that there are no objections to incorporating the notion of 'sincerity' or 'truthfulness' into the criterion; if this is done, then Mr. B's identification of a red object as 'red' will fail to satisfy the criterion for understanding even if, contrary to his inner convictions in the matter, he decides to 'go along with the game' and proceeds to identify objects which look blue to him as 'red' and so on. The claim then, will be, as we have seen, that Mr. B's performance does not satisfy the criterion for understanding and consequently that it is clear that he does not understand. Any claim that the fact that brain-waves from Mr. B's word-memory centers have not altered constitutes probabilistic evidence that he HAS retained an understanding of the color-words in question, will, by parity with Malcolm's argument, be dismissed, for it will be claimed that incorporation of brain-wave recordings as evidence constitutes in actuality the introduction of a *new* criterion of understanding, that the new concept thereby introduced is not our ordinary concept, and consequently that the sense in which Mr. B may be said to 'understand' is indeed an extraordinary and misleading one.

It is not difficult to construct an objection of the same sort against any claim that in circumstances in which others see a blue-colored object, Mr. B's experience is that of SEEING a red object, for supposing that there must exist a criterion on the basis of which color-experiences are ascribed, a NON-VERBAL test of ability to discriminate between various pigments may be construed as constituting the criterion for a person's SEEING, red, blue, green and so on, and Mr. B, by hypothesis, is able to do this. Supposing then, that an adherent of the outward-criterion doctrine holds that, on the basis of an appropriate non-verbal criterion, one is warranted in stating that Mr. B has the normal ability to discriminate between colors, it can then be argued that since Mr. B's performance satisfies THIS criterion, the color which he sees when placed in the blue room is our public color 'blue', that our ordinary concept 'blue' is the relevant concept here as elsewhere, and that the ascription 'sees a blue color' is warranted; the introduction of 'C-Waves' and the atypical condition of the subject's retinas as evidence to the contrary constitute in actuality the introduction of a NEW CRITERION, with the consequence that the expression "sees a blue color" is being used in a manner altogether different from its natural employment. It follows, then, on conceptual grounds, that retinal factors and brain-waves have nothing to do with whether or not Mr. B sees blue in the blue room.

The 'change-in-criteria-change-in meaning' account has undergone some severe criticism by a number of contemporary writers, as has the claim considered prior to it that justification for the ascription of psychological predicates must be criterion-dependent. I will now attempt to sketch out what appear to be some of the more telling objections which have been made against these claims.

Let us first consider the objection (2) that what appeared to be the introduction of evidence was actually an introduction of new criteria and that consequently the meanings of the expressions "understands the word 'blue' ", and "sees a blue color" have been altered by those who regard certain test results as evidence.

A preliminary question which perhaps should be noted is whether Malcolm (or Garver or Carney) would regard the meaning of all significant linguistic predicates as being ultimately criterion-governed. Within the scope of this paper it is not possible to do more than acknowledge the legitimate existence of such a question and to make a few suggestions: (A) In so far as one's approach to the matter is congruent with that of Wittgenstein, it seems evident that the application of color-predicates and other basic predicates used to describe physical objects (e.g., 'shape-predicates') would not be held to be criterion-governed.[8] (B) There exists a strong

---

[8] Ludwig Wittgenstein, *Philosophical Investigations* (New York, The Macmillan Company, 1953), Part I, section 381. The question as to whether I say something is red on the basis of a criterion is quite different from the question as to whether or not others attribute an understanding of the word 'red' to me, or judge that I see something red, on the basis of a criterion.

argument showing that an attempt to specify criteria governing the application of certain meaningful predicates other than those of the type (which one might call 'sense-datum' predicates) indicated in (A) must be a self-defeating enterprise, this being so, for example, in the case of the concepts 'true' and 'meaningful'.[9] One may conjecture that it might be admitted that the concepts of 'truth' and 'meaningfulness' are not criterion-governed without giving up the claim that psychological predicates are so governed, for it could be held that, e.g., the concepts 'true' and 'meaningful' have a role in the language whose character may be specified in some other illuminating manner.

For the purpose of the argument which follows, one is left free to suppose that there may be other sorts of predicates which Malcolm, or others holding to his view, would acknowledge are not criterion-governed; all that is necessary is that aMlcolm should hold that concepts in the domain of the natural sciences are criterion-governed, and that the criterion-meaning relationship in this domain is essentially the same as that which he alleges to hold in the domain of psychological predicates. The argument employed to show that there must be criterion for someone's having a sore foot can be applied *mutatis mutandis* to the case of something's being an acid or something's being a case of multiple sclerosis, and so on, namely that if there were no such thing as a criterion for something's being an acid or for something's being a case of poliomyelitis, no evidence for either could ever be obtained, in that the empirical correlations which would constitute evidence could never be established.

Mr. Hilary Putnam has noted that a 'change of meaning' account such as Malcolm's gives rise, in the realm of science, to some conclusions which one may find difficult to accept.[10] As one example Putnam has cited the development of techniques for the determination of chemical acidity. At an earlier time the only

[9] Robert J. Richman, "Concepts Without Criteria", *Theoria,* 31: 65-85, Part II (1965).

[10] Hilary Putnam, "Dreaming and Depth Grammar", *Analytical Philosophy: First Series,* R.J. Butler, ed. (New York, Barnes and Noble, 1962), 211-235.

known technique for making such determinations was effective within a comparatively restricted domain of compounds. Supposing that the concept 'acid' and with it the predicate 'is an acid' must have (then as now) been criterion-governed, the best available candidate for something constituting the governing criterion would have been the method of detection than available. By parity of situation one must suppose that present methods of detecting acidity constitute new criteria and that the meanings of 'acid' and 'is an acid' have thereby been changed. But this would make any statement by a chemist in the earlier epoch, that he expected that a better method of detecting acidity (one which would have application to a wider range of compounds) would eventually be found, an expression of conceptual confusion. Similarly, any statement by a contemporary chemist that the early techniques for determination of acidity were inferior to those currently in use would also be an expression of confusion, for applying the view expressed by Malcolm, the meanings of 'acid' and 'is an acid' were different in the earlier epoch, such that in the announcement that a new and far more sensitive technique for determining acidity has been discovered is to inaugurate a new (extraordinary and misleading?) use of the term 'acidity'. Malcolm's account, if true, would leave one with a rather strange version of what is actually involved in various areas of scientific progress, for such objectives as finding a better method of detecting acidity would, on Malcolm's account, be conceptually confused in the form in which they are generally understood.

It is not impossible that a conceptually confused inquiry should RESULT in an increase of knowledge, but on Malcolm's account even the successful results of such enterprises are not properly understood — scientists should properly be proclaiming, e.g., that a new concept of 'acidity' has been introduced or, upon discovery of a virus origin for poliomyelitis, that a new concept of 'polio' has been introduced into the field of pathology, rather than a confused claim that the pathogenic agent in this ancient disease has been discovered, or that, on the basis of improved diagnosis afforded by our knowledge of the polio virus, it has been discovered that there are sublinical cases of polio in which the characteristic syndrome of symptoms is not manifested.

This is not to say that concepts in science are necessarily immutable, but it seems clear that Malcolm's 'change-of-criterion-change-of-meaning' account would fail to furnish one with a correct understanding of such changes. If one were to inquire of an informed research pathologist whether the concept of 'polio' changed with the discovery of its virus origin, it may be supposed that such a person could reply that in the sense that we now have a better understanding of the nature of this disease, our concept of 'polio' is now a more sophisticated one, and IN THAT SENSE, may be said to have changed; but it is reasonable to suppose also that such a person would hold that the disease called 'polio' which formerly could be detected only through recognition of a syndrome of symptoms and the disease 'polio' presently detectable through identification of a particular virus are ONE AND THE SAME DISEASE, and that in this most essential respect the concept is the same today as formerly.

Note that the sense in which a pathologist might say that the concept of polio has changed is not a sense which accommodates itself to Malcolm's view; rather it is the sort of statement which, e.g., persons engaged in dream research, such as Dement and Kleitman, could, consistently with their own view of the matter, make, for they could say, like the pathologist, that in the sense that we now have a more complete understanding of the phenomenon called 'dreaming', our concept of this phenomenon may be said to have changed (improved) but that by 'dreams' they mean the same thing as anyone having a mastery of the language.

The above suggests that the accounts which would be given by intelligent persons actually working in various fields may be expected to yield a more illuminating account concerning 'change of concepts' having special relevance to a particular scientific endeavor than an account stemming from a philosophical theory of the type propounded by Malcolm. One wonders how a lexicographer would fare should he choose to orient his procedure to Malcolm's theory. If the above objections to Malcolm's 'change-in-meaning' account are cogent, by parity of reasoning it follows a 'change-in-meaning' objection to the incorporation of physiological facts as evidence for an instantiation of the inverted-spectrum hypothesis should be rejected.

Remaining for consideration is the allied objection (1) that any account arguing for the plausibility of a claim that Mr. B's color-experiences are transposed must be self-defeating in that such an account must presuppose that we do not have (conceptually-connected) criteria justifying the ascription of psychological predicates, said absence of criteria in turn obviating any possibility of empirical justification for claiming either that Mr. B understands the word 'blue' or that Mr. B's color-experiences are of a particular sort.

It can be shown that this objection is exceedingly weak, since the account of the nature of empirical justification involved is one which would exclude from the domain of 'non-psychological' knowledge a great deal which (rational) scientists do regard as justified hypotheses, and further that such an account fails to furnish one with so much as an inkling of the rationale underlying a great many experimental situations. These points have been the subject of some extensive discussions which I will not attempt to reproduce in complete form, but it may be wortwhile to mention an example cited by Chihara and Fodor,[11] namely C. T. W. Wilson's cloud-chamber. The justification for our belief that tracks in the cloud-chamber indicate the passage of ionized particles through the chamber cannot be accommodated to a 'criterion' account of justification, for there is in the nature of the cloud-chamber case, nothing which would qualify as a criterion for 'ionised particle' or 'path of ionized particle', or whatever, to which the cloud-chamber tracks could be (directly or indirectly) correlated; rather the justification for this interpretation rests upon a refined and complex body of antecedent theory developed and confirmed in the course of prior investigations in the field of physics. To regard the criterion

[11] C.S. Chihara and J.A. Fodor, "Operationalism and Ordinary Language: A Critique of Wittgenstein", *The American Philosophical Quarterly,* 2: 281-295 (1965).

account as an all-inclusive model of rational justification would entail not only giving up the claim that the account given by physicists of what is going on in the cloud-chamber is an explanation for which there is a rational justification, but also would leave us with the conclusion that Wilson's construction of the original cloud-chamber must have stemmed from some sort of conceptual confusion on his part.[12] To sum up, it is being argued that the account of justification adhered to by Malcolm is an unduly restricted account, and that an objection to the inverted-spectrum hypothesis which stems from it can be rejected on sound rational grounds; it may be added that should someone acknowledge the force of the above objections in the domain of non-psychological studies, but hold that the criterion account of justification is nevertheless the only defensible account with respect to psychological matters, it would be incumbent upon him to illuminate the special character of psychological subject-matter which justifies a contention that the criterion account is the only one having rational application. Since, to my knowledge, no explanation invulnerable to objections of the sort suggested by the Wilson cloud-chamber example has been advanced, it is difficult to anticipate what sort of an answer might be given.

Before proceeding farther, it may be advisable to sum up what has been said thus far: The starting point for the present discussion was the claim, on behalf of the anti-private-language thesis, that, in the absence of any observable behavioral or circumstantial phenomena associated with diary-keeper's alleged sensation, 'E' could not be or become a sensation-word, for sensation-words are ALTOGETHER dependent on publicly-observable phenomenae for their meaning (the outward-criterion doctrine). It was then noted that it would be a consequence of the truth of the outward-criterion doctrine that the inverted-spectrum hypothesis, together with all simplified variants, must be ruled out on conceptual grounds, i.e., that the truth of the outward-criterion doctrine would render the

[12] Just as, on Malcolm's view, it must be held that the experimental design set up by Dement and Kleitman would not have come into being in the absence of conceptual confusion.

inverted-spectrum hypothesis unintelligible. It has been argued that the inverted-spectrum hypothesis cannot be ruled out on conceptual grounds without doing violence to the body of psychological theory which we presently have, for it is congruent with this body of theory to suppose that empirical evidence constituting support for a hypothesis that transposition of color-experience has, in a particular case, actually occurred could in fact be gathered.

Two sorts of objections to the claim that evidence for transposed color-experience (in the hypothetical case considered) could in principle be obtained have been considered and rejected. The objection (1) that the notion of 'evidence' is defective in a claim for evidence of this sort, in that the evidence suggested does not link up with conceptually-connected criteria, has been rejected, since the theory of justification which gives rise to it is simplistic and too restricted to accommodate the developed and fruitful methodology actually employed in scientific investigation. The other objection (2) that a change of meaning of crucial psychological predicates would be involved in any claim that one had evidence for an instantiation of the inverted-spectrum hypothesis or some simplified variant has been rejected on the grounds that the 'change-of-criterion-change-of-meaning' account from which it stems would yield conclusions at variance with the judgment of those actually employing scientific concepts to which such a doctrine would have application; acceptance of the 'change-of-criterion-change-of-meaning' account would entail the conclusion that an incredible amount of disguised conceptual confusion exists in such non-esoteric fields as chemistry and pathology. It has been argued that such a doctrine contains nothing which would recommend it — that it affords no useful insights, is gratuitous and untrue. It has been suggested that something approaching an illuminating account of conceptual change could be obtained through discussion with intelligent persons having a good knowledge of the field of endeavor in which the relevant concept plays a role, and that such accounts would not, in a great many cases, accord with the results of Malcolm's method. Therefore it is argued that the inverted-spectrum hypothesis is intelligible and that this fact indicates that the outward-criterion doctrine gives a defective account of the sensation-word-meaning relationship. This being so, the objection that 'E', in virtue of the absence of criterial behavior and circumstances, must be ruled out as a possible sensation-word is unsubstantiated, and so the third argument presented in Mr. Garver's paper in support of the anti-private-language thesis must be judged a failure.

Admittedly one may have reservations concerning the intelligibility of the inverted-spectrum hypothesis on grounds OTHER than those afforded by the outward-criterion doctrine; if reasonable objections exist which warrant the rejection of the view that the inverted-spectrum hypothesis describes a possible state-of-affairs, then something is amiss in the argument I have employed to show that the hypothesis is intelligible.

Although it is not possible to enter into a comprehensive consideration of the sorts of objections which suggest themselves, an attempt will be made to show that some of the more obvious objections which might be advanced are not as effective as would appear at first glance. At least three objections may be readily anticipated; these are:

(1) If the inverted-spectrum hypothesis is intelligible, then it may be that each of us means something different by the word 'red'; this means that we may be failing to communicate in our employment of color-words.

(2) If it is intelligible to suppose that what another calls 'red' I have learned to call 'blue' then, by parity of reasoning, there is no reason to suppose that the same could not hold with respect to 'shape-words', and the latter is manifestly absurd.

(3) If the inverted-spectrum hypothesis is held to be intelligible, it seems that a similar argument can be constructed to show that the same holds true for bodily sensations, and that, e.g., what one person calls a sensation of pain may be the sensation which another has learned to call a tickling sensation; this is an absurdity.

It must, on the view being presented, be acknowledged that the objection (or perhaps, 'reservation') expressed in (1) does indicate a consequence of the claim that the inverted-spectrum is a logical possibility; however, it expresses a consequence which is subject to certain qualifications.

First, it is easy to see that, in what may be called an 'operational' (or pragmatic) sense there would be no failure of communication, provided that Mr. B decided to bring his employment of the relevant color-words into conformity with their general employment, for having done so, his request that someone bring him a red blanket will have reference to the same kind of blanket that others call 'red'. On the other hand, provided one has an understanding of Mr. B's situation, one will be able to understand his statement that his own perceptual experience in looking at the red blanket is that of seeing a blue blanket, i.e., in what we may choose to call the EXPERIENTIAL sense of the word, the blanket in question appears to him to be blue in color.

It seems then, that in a case like that of Mr. B there need be no failure of communication. However, it also appears to be the case that (philosophically unwelcome though this may be,) our claim that the inverted-spectrum hypothesis is intelligible does ALLOW for the possibility of failure of communication in the 'experiential' sense; for we are free to imagine that research scientists might discover someone who has never had the disease caused by 'virus X', but whose retinas contain factor 'Y' in place of factor 'X' and whose brain-waves in the relevant tests are of the same character as those manifested by Mr. B. Suppose such an individual, call him 'Mr. C', replies, in response to questions, that he has never noticed any alteration, in the requisite sense, of his experiences of color. On the basis of the psychological and perceptual theory in virtue of which transposition of certain experiences of color is suspected in the case of Mr. B, we have warrant for supposing that a similar transposition is instantiated in the case of Mr. C. If this is so, then it would seem to follow that in an 'experiential' sense, Mr. C's descriptions of colors and expressions of color-preferences have failed to communicate, for example in a disagreement with someone as to whether pale red or pale blue is a more pleasing or appropriate color in some type of interior decoration.

Second, supposing this failure of 'experiential' communication to be a LOGICAL possibility in the case of color-predicates, any supposition that this may actually be the case, would be warranted only to the extent that evidence for this hypothesis is available. *Prima facie*, there is at least one feature of our world which may count against such a supposition, *viz.*, that IF our rather general agreement that some colors are appropriately characterized as 'gay' or 'cheerful', others as 'somber', and others as 'warm' is best accounted for as expressing natural reactions to color-experience rather than as expressing learned reactions (this is a question for psychology), then the simplest explanation for this general agreement in natural response is that those who agree in their appraisal of, e.g., 'canary yellow' as being a cheerful color appropriate for kitchen decoration, have the same sort of visual experience when looking at 'canary yellow'.

However, even supposing that a 'cultural convention' account should prove to be a better psychological explanation for the above-noted agreement, one still has no POSITIVE ground for supposing, e.g., that there ARE genetically caused instantiations of the inverted-spectrum hypothesis, and in the absence of some positive grounds, such as those indicated in the hypothetical case considered, for supposing the inverted-spectrum hypothesis to be instantiated, the supposition that it IS so (with its consequence that there are 'radical' experiential failures in communications involving color-predicates) may be intellectually entertaining (or dismaying) but it is also completely gratuitous. In appraising such a possibility a methodological directive suggested by Hilary Putnam in his paper, "Brains and Behavior", is, in the judgment of the writer, eminently rational; Mr. Putnam's subject is 'pain', but the principle stated is susceptible to generalization:

If some organism is in the same state as a human being in pain in all respects KNOWN to be relevant, and there is no reason to suppose that there exist UNKNOWN relevant aspects, then don't postulate any.[13]

The second anticipated objection is perhaps more difficult to deal with, for one may well have some difficulty in conceiving a system-

---

[13] Hilary Putnam, "Brains and Behavior", *Analytical Philosophy: Second Series*, R.J. Butler, ed. (Oxford, Basil Blackwell, 1965), 19.

atic distortion of perceptual experience which would have as its consequence the application of the predicate 'is square in shape' to objects which 'experientially' appear round in shape to the perceiver and *vice-versa*. However, it is worth noting that one necessary precondition for such a possibility, namely the possibility of consistent distortion of perceived shapes is one which we all accept, one example of such a condition being astigmatism, another being those rare cases in which psychologists have reason to believe that the subject has a defect in his perceptual apparatus causing him to see objects 'upside down'. However, such distortions have behavioral consequences, and what is to be imagined is a type of distortion in which, at least in a 'genetic' case, no such consequences would be manifested. If it is possible to construct a coherent picture of such a perceptual world, that is, depict the circumstances in virtue of which no behavioral indicators would be evident, then it seems to follow that the LOGICAL possibility that, e.g., round objects appear square to someone and square objects round, would have to be admitted. I find it impossible to conceive of how such an account could be spelled out in an intelligible manner;[14] however, even supposing that it could be done, one would still, in the absence of any evidence for it, have absolutely no reason to suppose that such instantiations exist, and this for the same reasons indicated in the discussion of the first objection.

The third anticipated objection has perhaps the greatest appearance of strength, for one finds something exceedingly strange that someone might be calling 'pain' what I call 'tickling'. Admittedly, the supposition is absurd, but the absurdity is not, on the view here being advocated, of a CONCEPTUAL nature.

It would seem that consistency requires the logical possibility of such a case, provided one is able to retain the concept of a human being in so doing, and this is not an easy task. Regarding the causes of pain as contingently related to the occurrence of pain, perhaps

---

[14] E.g., what would a game of billiards look like to such a person? What would determine the location of the corners on the billiard-balls, and wouldn't it strike him as strange that the language had no words referring to the geome trical elements (corners and planes) of billiard-balls?

it is possible to construct a hypothetical case such as that of a cunning child-masochist who giggles upon being tickled (which causes pain IN HIM) and comes back for more of the same, and who, in the case of touching the hot stove, though finding the sensation to be a pleasant tickling, invariably undergoes a seizure of pain-behavior over which he has no control, and to elaborate this into the fantastic degree of complexity in order to cover all situations, but supposing such a hypothesis could be constructed, one would have nothing more than a completely mad story on a level with that of an explanation given by a psychotic as to how it is that he, the only descendant of the lost Dauphin, has been incarcerated by political enemies who plan to poison him. The mere logical possibility of the psychotic's story does not, in itself, make the truth of such an account at all likely.

The absence of a criterial relation does not make one explanation as good as another. Suppose scientists have placed a cloud-chamber in an experimental situation in which there is reason to suppose that the paths of two types of particles, call them 'alpha' and 'beta', will be manifested, and that their antecedent theory gives them every reason to suppose that, under the test conditions being inaugurated, alpha particles will show curved paths and beta particles will show straight paths, and that no other kinds of streak-producing particles will be passing through the chamber. If the curved paths and straight paths show up as expected, an objection that it is logically possible that in THIS experiment the alpha particles are producing straight paths and the beta particles curved paths would be dismissed — it would not be incumbent on the experimenters to produce proof that abnormal causal factors did not exist, provided there existed in fact no reason to suppose such to be true. A super-skeptic might point out that it is logically possible that an evil demon or a mischievous super-scientist operating from a distance might be altering the paths of the particles in a systematic way, but even granting such a hypothesis to be intelligible, it would serve to cast no real doubt on the experimental proceedings; it would amount to no more than a silly suggestion which one would have no reason to believe to be true.

VIII

CRITERIA AND MRS. THOMSON'S 'STEP THREE'

In discussing Mrs. Thomson's attempt to exhibit the logical bones of the first argument considered, it was suggested that those who have advanced this argument for the anti-private-language thesis subscribe to some general doctrine concerning the nature of language and meaning which constitutes an effective equivalent of what Mrs. Thomson found to be 'step three' of the argument.

Prior to indicating the sort of account which (1) would constitute an effective equivalent of the 'third step' and which (2) appears to be compatible with certain views expressed by those presenting arguments for the anti-private-language thesis, it may be worthwhile to re-present Mrs. Thomson's version of what the general argument amounts to. On Mrs. Thomson's analysis, the skeleton of the argument can be stated as follows:

(1) If a sign 'K' which a man uses is to be a name of a kind of thing in a language, his use of it must be governed by a rule of the form, X's and only X's are to be called 'K's'.

(2) If a sign 'K' which a man uses is to be a kind-name in a language, then it must be possible that he should call a thing 'K' thinking it is an X when it is not an X, when it is the X's and only the X's which (in his use) are to be called 'K's'.

(3) There is no such thing as a man's thinking a thing is of a kind to be called 'K' and its not being so unless it is logically possible that it be found out that it is not so.[1]

With the addition of a fourth statement, namely one to the effect

---

[1] Judith Jarvis Thomson, "Private Languages", *The American Philosophical Quarterly*, 1: 23-27 (1964).

that in the case of the diary-keeper it is NOT logically possible for anyone (including the diary-keeper) to find out whether or not he has made such an unwitting mistake, the conclusion that 'E' cannot be a sign in a language follows.

Now the question at hand concerns what sort of justification is available, for a proponent of the anti-private-language thesis, for step three or some effective variant of step three. I want to suggest that an account such as the following indicates the sorts of considerations which have formed a partially implicit element in the argument considered by Mrs. Thomson, this being so because, on the account to be suggested, all that is required for support of step three is the following claim:

Sensation-words, construed as kind-names, must belong to the class of those kind-names requiring criteria of application as a necessary condition for meaning.

If the above claim is held to be true, then it is not difficult to construct an argument justifying step three. This can be done in the following way. First, for the sake of simplicity, step three may be re-stated as follows:

It is logically possible to mistakenly identify something as a K only if it is logically possible to find out that it is not a K.

Letting 'K' stand for any kind-name in the class of criterion-governed kind-names the argument for the above claim can be formulated in the following manner:

(A) It is logically possible to identify something as a K mistakenly only if it is logically possible to identify something as a K correctly.
(B) It is logically possible to identify something as a K correctly only if the sign 'K' has meaning.
(C) 'K' has meaning only if there are criteria governing the application of 'K'.
(D) There are criteria governing the application of 'K' only if it is logically possible to find out that something is not a K.

By transitivity of the relations, the antecedent of (A) implies the consequent of (D) and a justification for the third step has been given. It is easy to see that by appropriate amendment of the statements involved, the same sort of argument may be formulated to yield the verbatim formulation of Mrs. Thomson's third step, or some other version which someone might regard as a more appropriate formulation such as, e.g.,

It makes sense to say that someone has misidentified something as a K only if it is possible (or, we know how in other cases) to find out that something is not a K.

The sort of justification suggested above is sound only if it is true that the ultimate justification for our second and third-person ascriptions of psychological predicates must consist of conceptually-connected criteria. It has been argued previously that the criterion account (1) is not the only account of justification available, since such a view is too restricted to encompass patterns of justificatory reasoning finding fruitful employment in the sciences, and (2) that such an account leads (e.g., in the case of the inverted-spectrum hypothesis) to conclusions both (a) counter-intuitive and (b) in conflict with conclusions warranted by application of sound scientific method. If the objections which have been advanced are sound, then the sort of justification suggested for Mrs. Thomson's step three is unsound, for premise 'C' is unsubstantiated.

On the assumption that what has been said thus far is essentially correct, it is now possible to obtain a clearer view of what is involved in the notion of a private language, in the sense intended by Malcolm, Garver and Carney. A private language, it will be recalled, was characterized as a (putative) language the words of which CANNOT (on one way of reading Malcolm this is to be a LOGICAL impossibility) be understood by anyone other than the person supposedly using the language, this being so BECAUSE the words of the private language refer to what can only be known to the speaker; to his 'immediate private sensations'.

Let us reconsider the situation of the hypothetical diary-keeper. The diary-keeper has undertaken to record the occurrences of a particular sensation for which, by hypothesis, there are no behavioral or circumstantial indicators constituting (conceptually connected) criteria. On the view of justification presented by Malcolm, the absence of criteria obviates the possibility of any probabilistic evidence that, say, last Tuesday the diary-keeper experienced a sensation of the same kind as that which he initially decided to call 'E', and this means that if I were to look at the diary and see an 'E' inscribed together with the appropriate date, I would have no reason to suppose that the diary-keeper had actually experienced E last Tuesday. But this claim, that I can never know WHEN the diary-keeper experiences E, in itself gives me no reason for concluding that I have NO understanding of what 'E' means, for I could say, "'E' is supposedly being used to record the occurrence of a certain kind of sensation — I have no way of knowing what kind of a sensation it may be, or whether, e.g., it did occur last Tuesday, but nevertheless I understand 'E' in THIS sense, namely that the diary-keeper is (or believes himself to be) using this sign to record the occurrence of a particular kind of sensation." In knowing that a mark is supposed to stand for a particular kind of sensation, one already has a partial understanding of it; cases in which we have NO understanding of a sign in a language are instantiated in the case of a dead language which we have no means of translating; supposing that records written in such a language contained a sign equivalent to the English word 'pain', we would have no way of knowing which sign it was, even to the extent of knowing that it was a sign for SOME kind of a sensation.

I am inclined to suggest that if it is allowed that we might understand this much about 'E' (that it is a sign for SOME kind of a sensation), there seems to be nothing which prevents us from coming to a better understanding, for, if we know that 'E' is supposedly being used to record the occurrence of a particular kind of sensation, why it is not intelligible to suppose that the diary-keeper could tell us (or claim) that "E" is being employed to record a peculiar kind of bodily sensation or visual experience? It may be held that since the diary-keeper hypothesis is so sketchily spelled out by those who have advanced the argument in which it plays a role, such a supposition is certainly allowable. However, whether or not it IS allowable is not especially important, since already it has been indicated that the criterion theory of JUSTIFICATION as applied to

50380

ascription of psychological predicates does not in itself obviate the possibility of SOME understanding of the sign 'E' on the part of persons other than the diary-keeper and, so 'E' is not in virtue of such a doctrine, a sign which, in any strict sense, others cannot understand.

If it is to be a logical impossibility for others to understand the sign 'E', it seems clear that the criterion account of justification not only does not obviate the possibility of a partial understanding on the part of others, it does not even preclude the possibility of a complete understanding, for, PER MALCOLM,[2] it is logically possible that someone might be born with an understanding, or that a drug might produce it in him, or that he might know through clairvoyance.

What gives rise to the logical impossibility of understanding 'E' is the criterion account of MEANING as applied to sensation-words (the outward-criterion doctrine) which states that the meaning of sensation-words is in no way dependent on anything one might call 'immediate private experiences', but rather is altogether dependent on (criterial) behavior and circumstances. As was briefly indicated previously, once such an account is accepted, it follows that it would be logically impossible for others to understand 'E' as a word referring to a particular kind of sensation since from the absence of criterial behavior and circumstances it follows that 'E' cannot be a word for a sensation.

Although it is the criterial account of MEANING which entails the logical impossibility of understanding the diary-keeper's 'E' as well as any other putative sign supposedly having meaning through being associated with an immediate private sensation, it is not accidental that one advancing the anti-private-language thesis, e.g., Malcolm, will also subscribe to a criterial theory of JUSTIFICATION for, the criterial account of justification supports the criterial account of how it is that sensation-words and other psychological terms have meaning in the following way: If it is

[2] Norman Malcolm, "Wittgenstein's *Philosophical Investigations*", *The Philosophy of Mind,* V.C. Chappell, ed. (Englewood Cliffs, N.J, Prentice-Hall, 1962), 86.

true that we are sometimes justified in ascribing, e.g., pains and dreams to others AND if it is true that the only legitimate sort of justification in these matters must be of a kind ultimately resting on conceptually-connected criteria consisting of relevant behavior and circumstances, then the outward-criterion doctrine follows, for the character of immediate private mental whatnots becomes irrelevant to the kind of warrant justifying such ascriptions; sensation-words have the meaning which they do have only in virtue of a conceptual connection with behavior and circumstances.

IX

CONCLUSION

Since it has been argued that the outward-criterion doctrine is incorrect, it may be in order to suggest, in greater detail than has been done thus far, an account which (1) is capable of accommodating the inverted-spectrum hypothesis, and which (2) allows for the possibility of justifying ascriptions of sensations and other psychological events to others without necessitating the postulation of conceptually-connected criteria.

Suggestions forming the basis for what appears to be a more plausible account are contained in the previously-cited paper by Chihara and Fodor, a paper which contains a considerably more elaborated account than will be presented here.[1] The nub of this account consists of the suggestion that psychological concepts have a role significantly similar to certain concepts playing a crucial role in the physical sciences. For example, the concept 'pain' may be fruitfully construed as being similar in some essential respects to that of 'ionized particle' in the following way: On the basis of another's behavior and circumstances, one has warrant for ascribing pain to that person; on the basis of the appearance of a track in the Wilson cloud-chamber, the observer of this track has warrant for believing (or knows) that an ionized particle has passed through the chamber. In both cases the judgment made is justified, not by means of some ultimate conceptually-connected criterion governing application of the relevant terms ('pain' and

[1] C.S. Chihara and J.A. Fodor, "Operationalism and Ordinary Language: A Critique of Wittgenstein", *The American Philosophical Quarterly*, 4: 281-295 (1965).

'ionized particle') but rather on the basis of an antecedent body of theory which has a fruitful explanatory and predictive power. The relationship between pain and pain-behavior is of the same general sort as that obtaining between an ionized particle and the cloud-chamber track; pain-behavior and cloud-chamber tracks indicate the existence of a something which is not independently identifiable, and they do so, not by means of some conceptual connection to the relevant concepts, but rather through their connection to the postulated features of the minds of others in the former case and the world of physics in the latter. Pain-behavior and cloud-chamber tracks have the status of contingently-connected indicators.

The above sort of account is capable of accommodating the inverted-spectrum hypothesis as a logical possibility, and it also allows for the possibility of evidence that the inverted spectrum has actually been instantiated; it was implicitly presupposed in the previous discussion concerning the logical possibility of the inverted spectrum together with the possibility of evidence for it. On the view being advocated, sensation-words and certain other psychological terms, refer in a quite straightforward sense, to elements of immediate sensory experience. On this view it is perfectly intelligible, in the case of Mr. B, to question whether he, in looking at a patch covered with a particular pigment, is having the same sort of visual experience as oneself or others having normal eyesight in the relevant respects. It is also allowed that evidence for the existence of atypical private experiences is a possibility, such evidence being behavioral and physiological facts tying into our psychological theory in virtue of what might be called their 'operational fit'.

Admittedly the above constitutes no more than a suggestion as to the sort of role played by a certain class of psychological terms, perhaps difficult to delimit, but of which 'pain', 'seeing' and 'dream'[2] furnish examples. There is, however, one further matter

---

[2] It is not implied that in the use of these terms, one is referring only to immediate sensory contents; dreams, for example, consist of more than sensory content in that conceptual articulation is involved.

in connection with these terms, that of meaning and denotation, which perhaps should be mentioned.

To begin, let us reconsider a previously-cited statement by Mr. Garver, which was:

... 'pain' depends upon pain-behavior rather than on any inner private experience for its meaning.[3]

Two alternatives are indicated in the above statement, one being the outward-criterion doctrine, the other being a claim that such words as 'pain' and 'dream' depend upon 'inner private experiences' for their meaning. I want to suggest that the latter alternative expressed by Mr. Garver may, in the form in which it is stated, be somewhat misleading. On the view being suggested 'pain' and 'dream' are denoting terms, but it is NOT NECESSARY, considering these terms separately, that there be any instantiations of that which the term purports to denote in order for the particular term to have meaning. The case of 'pain' and 'dream', in this respect may be compared to that of 'phlogiston'. The word 'phlogiston' was at one time in the history of science regarded as the name of a particular kind of material substance; however, we now know that such a substance does not exist. Nevertheless the word 'phlogiston' has meaning even though no such substance has ever existed. 'Phlogiston' obviously does not depend upon the existence of phlogiston for its meaning and similarly 'pain' and 'dream' do not depend on the existence of pains and dreams ('inner private experiences') for their meaning.

Someone inclined to regard the comparison with 'phlogiston' to be essentially sound may suspect that the unwelcome consequence that 'pain' and 'dream' may also have no instantiations follows, since such instantiations are not essential to their having the meanings they do have. This is a rather difficult suggestion to deal with, and I find it possible to do no more with it than advance a few suggestions. Let us suppose that a man, call him 'Mr. D', is born without the capacity to experience physical pain;

[3] Newton Garver, "Wittgenstein on Private Language", *Philosophy and Phenomenological Research,* 20: 391 (1960).

that none of the normal causes of pain produced this type of sensation in him would be evident from his behavior. There is no reason to suppose that such a man, having a normal INTELLECTUAL endowment, could not come to understand the word 'pain' and ascribe it to others in appropriate circumstances. He could understand an explanation that pain is an unpleasant kind of bodily sensation usually caused by events damaging to the organism such as blows, excessive heat, cutting, etc., which, when severe, often causes such behavior as crying, wincing, groaning, writhing, screaming, swearing, etc.

It is certainly possible that long before the advent of Lavoisier's theory of the nature of combustion, it occurred to some sceptical chemist that, even though the existence of phlogiston furnished a seemingly reasonable explanation of the process of combustion, it might be the case that there was in fact no such substance as phlogiston. Suppose Mr. D has a similar kind of doubt concerning the alleged sensation, pain, namely that although the existence of such a sensation seems to furnish a good explanation of certain aspects of the behavior of others, it is logically possible that there might in fact be no such sensation. Such a doubt by Mr. D would not, on the view being advocated, be, considered in itself, CONCEPTUALLY incoherent; however, it would be a reasonable doubt only if some sort of plausible justification for it could be developed by Mr. D.

Could Mr. D retain even THIS doubt once he had experienced pain himself? Let us suppose that his physician detects a genetically-caused abnormality in Mr. D and proceeds to correct it, and that after the condition is corrected, Mr. D notes a significant change in the character of his experiences — he touches the hot stove and experiences a violently unpleasant sensation which causes him to clutch the burned hand, grit his teeth, grimace, swear violently and hope fervently that the sensation will soon pass. Can he now doubt that the word 'pain' has at least one referent? It would be reasonable for him to suppose that what he had experienced was a case of pain, since by hypothesis he understands the explanation of the word 'pain' indicated above, but could he, the arch-sceptic, object that it is logically possible that it was some other sort of previously unencountered sensation whose unpleasant qualities caused him to behave in such a manner? On the general view here being advocated, it seems that such a Cartesian doubt would not be (again, in itself,) CONCEPTUALLY incoherent, but it would be groundless in the absence of any reasonable considerations supporting it. This is not to suggest that any real possibility of a mistaken identification by Mr. D of a kind of bodily sensation previously unexperienced by him should be ruled out *a priori.* It is not unreasonable, for example, to conjecture that a person in circumstances like those of Mr. D might mistake the sensation produced by his first electrical shock as an instance of pain, provided he were ignorant of the precise cause of the experience in question, and had not yet experienced any instances of pain. Note that in the circumstances described it would be the case that a person understands the meaning of 'pain' and nevertheless makes a mistake in identifying his own sensation as a pain.

It seems evident that the account being suggested as a reasonable alternative is not capable of annihilating the ghost of Cartesian scepticism, but I want to suggest that this is not necessarily a serious defect. First, to my knowledge we have no good reasons for supposing it to be true that others do not have experiences, or that their experiences are radically unlike our own, and second, the supposition that others do have experiences and that these experiences are substantially like our own has an explanatory power with reference to the behavior of others which, in the absence of a better explanation, it is unreasonable to question seriously.

In this connection, I want to suggest that there is a strong 'Cartesian' element in the philosophic approach which underlies the anti-private-language thesis. The thesis is one consequence of an attempt to inter, with absolute finality, the 'problem of other minds'. Probabilistic reasoning, together with the absence of any evidence to the contrary, is not good enough; rather the DESI-DERATUM is something which will show that any philosophic doubt concerning the existence of sensations, thoughts and feelings in others, must, at bottom, be conceptually incoherent, the verbal expression of which can refer to no possible state-of-affairs. The criterion account of meaning applied to psychological terms, would, if correct, entail that there is no such thing as an intelligible doubt concerning the existence of other minds, for, if the outward-criterion doctrine were a correct account, such a doubt could not be intelligibly expressed in our language, and, provided that the limits of language coincide with the limits of rational thought, a doubt concerning the existence of other minds would be, at bottom, unintelligible, and someone who believed such a doubt to be intelligible could, at least in principle, be shown the way out of the unrecognized conceptual confusion which gave rise to the pseudo-question. (Descartes shows me that my doubt implies the conceptually incoherent consequence that God must be a deceiver, and so it follows that ...).

The above remarks are not intended as a disparagement of those who have advanced the anti-private-language thesis or of Wittgenstein to whom the claim in question is often attributed. Resolving the problem of other minds is a legitimate objective, and the intellectual resourcefulness exhibited in the attempted solution is impressive. One worthwhile legacy from the efforts of Wittgenstein, and others influenced by him in relevant respects should be a prudent restraining of a simplistic tendency to regard ALL psychological predicates as denoting elements of 'private experience'. Acknowledging that the program in question has yielded some not inconsiderable benefits for philosophy, it nevertheless must, as far as I am able to determine, be judged a failure with respect to its intended objective, and with it the anti-private-language thesis, being so intimately connected (no criterion, no psychological concept), also fails. Concerning the problem of other minds, it may be best to begin, as Peirce admonishes us to do, with acknowledging the beliefs we already have, and then, if possible, to give a rational account of them, refine them, and hopefully, arrive at a better understanding of an important feature of our world.

Prior to bringing this discussion to a close, I should like to mention three further matters which may be worth some attention. First, it may be objected that if certain psychological predicates are construed as denoting elements of private experience, it becomes a complete mystery as to how a child could ever come to employ these terms correctly. Second and third, it may be that something should be said concerning the consequences of the view being suggested (admittedly in rudimentary form) for epistemology and metaphysics.

An objection that children would not be able to learn the correct application of psychological predicates if the view being suggested were correct constitutes a claim that a philosophical theory stands in contradiction to an empirical fact. It seems likely that the most effective rebuttal would be one which could (supposing that it could) be given by someone specializing in the study of learning-patterns and concept-formation in normal children. Since the writer lacks such qualifications what will be said on this subject will be somewhat restricted.

First, the proposal that there are some fundamental logical similarities between the concepts 'pain' and 'dream' on the one hand, and 'phlogiston' and 'ionized particle' on the other, may cause the former concepts to appear to be more sophisticated than is actually the case, for the latter would not be well-understood in the absence of a considerable amount of antecedent concept-formation. For instance, one might show a four-year-old the Wilson Cloud-Chamber and, pointing to a newly-formed streak, say, "See, an ionized particle made that streak", and, perhaps, if the child were interested in this new object, the cloud chamber, he could soon answer the question (as we point to a streak), "What did that?", with "Ionized particle" (further success: Mamma comes along and Peter says, as a streak appears, "See Mamma — ionized particle did it!"). Perhaps the matter could be made intelligible to the four-year-old to the extent that his declarations would be something more than parrot-like utterances ("a tiny something so small we can't see it makes the streak, just like ..."), but in the absence of some comprehension of related concepts and theory, a four-year-old's understanding of what produced the streak would be exceedingly limited. (Another Peter, three centuries earlier, points to the fire and says, "See Mamma — the phlogiston is going away!")

The case of 'pain', is not, on the view being suggested, radically different, although the antecedent concept formation necessary for an understanding of this term is not as sophisticated and complex. It is logically possible that one could teach a child to say "The dog's foot hurts", in the appropriate circumstances, prior to his coming to UNDERSTAND what the sentence means, since a parrot could be trained to utter this sentence whenever the family dog came into view limping with a sore foot, and this would not show us that the parrot understood the sentence. On the view being advocated, correct use of new psychological concepts normally coincides with the development of a conceptual scheme adequate to integrate the concept involved, and the fact that some psychological terms are normally learned earlier than others indicates that concepts acquired earlier may furnish the logical prerequisites for subsequent assimilation of more sophisticated concepts. Whether or not normal children would be able to master the concepts "pain" and "dream" at the age in which they in fact do, supposing the above account to be correct, is not something to be decided *a priori*, but rather by attending to the psychological learning-theory best able to account for the relevant empirical facts about child-development.

Parenthetically, perhaps a few words are in order on the subject of 'understanding'. It may be objected that the notion of 'understanding' is none too clear in the above discussion, and that it is not evident, on the view being presented that 'understanding' must be withheld from the hypothetical parrot, for, supposing there are no conceptually-connected CRITERIA for understanding, it must be that 'understanding' is supposed to refer to some sort of inner private experience, and, supposing this to be the case, isn't it logically possible that, e.g., the hypothetical parrot might understand the sentence he utters in the appropriate circumstances?

The reply to this is that (1) it is not necessary, on the view being advocated, to construe ALL psychological predicates as denoting bits of inner private experience, and (2) that, although there are no conceptually-connected criteria for understanding, there ARE probabilistic indicators which, linking up with the perhaps partially implicit psychological theory which, in rudimentary form at least, is our common pre-academic inheritance, are more often than not rationally and practically decisive. On the basis of such contingently-connected indicators we attribute understanding to the child as he responds to statements employing the crucial term in appropriate ways, and what he does and says constitutes the basis for attributing the relevant degree of understanding. One crucial way in which the normal parrot differs from the normal child is that children, unlike parrots, fairly early in the process of mastering the language begin to utter novel sentences (sentences which they have never heard) in circumstances appropriate to the requesting, demanding, complaining or simply declarative statements being uttered for the first time. The most appropriate explanation for such facts is that the child has a conscious developing mind in which new concepts, as well as inductive and deductive capacities, are being formed in response to developing experience containing (as in one's own experience) some repetitive elements. The normal parrot does not develop novel and appropriate sentences in this way. Granted, he may accidently juxtapose fragments of previously-learned sentences into a new grammatical sentence, but circumstances will indicate that the new sentence resulted from random juxtaposition. True, if a particular parrot's linguistic development parallelled that of a normal child, one would have warrant for attributing understanding of the relevant concepts to the bird in this sense, namely that a null-hypothesis to the effect that the parrot's timely and appropriate discourse was simply due to the operation of chance factors in the juxtaposition of learned linguistic fragments would be simply incredible (though logically possible). The parrot's apparent mastery of the language might not force one to the conclusion that the parrot understood, for supposing an autopsy disclosed the parrot's brain to be no different from the standard parrot-brain in any detectible respect, in an effort to preserve a segment of psychological theory concerning the relationship obtaining between brains and intelligence, one might (reluctantly) resort to the null-hypothesis, or perhaps seek for an explanation ruling out both the truth of the propositions comprising 'P' in Chapter I, or propositions very much like them.[5]

If the views underlying the anti-private-language thesis were correct, it appears to follow, as Malcolm and others have claimed, that such enterprises as sense-data theory and phenomenalistic programs must be rejected as radically misconceived, for terms purporting to stand for elements of immediate (private) experience would be in the alleged circumstances of the hypothetical diary-keeper's 'E' since, first, sense-datum expressions cannot be construed as referring, on anything like the model of 'object and name', to elements of immediate sensory experience, and, second, even if, *per impossibile*, the connection between the experiential item and the sense-datum word were set up by one person, others could not (by any normal means) know what the referent of the sign in fact was, and an intersubjective meaning would not be possible; professor X's understanding of 'blue sense-datum' would only fortuitously be the same as student Y's.

If the arguments which have been advanced against the outward-criterion doctrine and for the intelligibility of the inverted-spectrum hypothesis are sufficiently cogent, then it follows the above-mentioned area of epistemology should not be rejected in order to accommodate the anti-private-language thesis, for it has not been shown that something like the model of 'object and name' is inappropriate with respect to sense-datum words, and, as has been previously argued, in the absence of any evidence indicating that one person's immediate experience differs radically from that or another in the same circumstances, we have no reason to believe that an expression such as 'blue sense-data', or some more fortunately expressed equivalent, does not convey the intended meaning from one person to another.

I wish to turn, for a brief moment, to an area of philosophy generally characterized as metaphysical in order to anticipate a possible claim that the general argument in this paper is an argument for Cartesian dualism, or something very much like it.

---

[5] Above, p. 16f.

In reply to this it must be acknowledged that the general argument is compatible with a metaphysical dualism of the Cartesian sort, although it is, in at least one respect, not compatible with the original thesis of Descartes, since, if the existence of immediate sensory experience is to be accounted for by means of postulating mental substances, 'psychoids', or whatever, one has no reason for withholding such an item from any organism whose behavior indicates the existence of sensory awareness, and so cats and bees will, by parity of situation, be invested with a dualistic nature also. However, it should be noted that the intelligibility of the inverted-spectrum hypothesis, upon which a substantial portion of argument in this paper may be said to rest, appears to be compatible with a number of competing accounts of psychophysical relationships such as epiphenomenalism, parallellism, and identity theory. There are, it may be supposed, other types of accounts already developed or in the process of development which are compatible with the conclusions of this paper. Which compatible account is the most adequate or most plausible is a large question; I have no unique insights concerning this venerable problem. In substance, all that is being said here concerning the mind-body problem is that the account of the relation between immediate sensory experience and words purporting to denote or refer to items of such experience allows for the possibility of the intelligible FORMULATION of the mind-body problem, whereas the views underlying the anti-private-language thesis do not, for reasons substantially the same as those entailing the claimed unintelligibility of sense-data theory and phenomenalism; the account being suggested does not serve to indicate which, if any, existing account compatible with it is correct.

Now, finally, a backward glance at the initial question: Can there be a private language? If the arguments presented in this paper are cogent, the answer (as one might expect) depends upon what is meant by a 'private language'. If the question is whether a man could invent and use a sign to stand for and record the occurrence of an immediate private sensation having no behavioral indicators either contingent or criterial, the answer appears to be 'yes'. On the other hand, if the question is whether it is possible that a man could invent a sign of this kind which not only (a) is used by him to refer to such a sensation but which also (b) is logically impossible for others to understand, the answer is 'no', for if it is granted that the sign can be employed to refer to a sensation, then it has a meaning, and if a sign has meaning, then it is logically possible that others could come to understand it.

SELECTED BIBLIOGRAPHY

Ayer, A.J., "Can There be a Private Language?", *The Concept of a Person and Other Essays* (New York St. Martin's Press, 1963), 1-79.

Ayer, A.J., "Privacy", *The Concept of a Person and Other Essays* (New York, St. Martin's Press, 1963), 52-81.

Carney, James D., "Private Language: The Logic of Wittgenstein's Argument", *Mind*, 69 (1960), 560-565.

Castaneda, Hector-Neri, "The Private-Language Argument", *Knowledge and Experience: Proceedings of the 1962 Oberlin Colloquium in Philosophy*, C.D. Rollins, ed. (University of Pittsburgh Press), 88-105.

Chappell, V.C., "Comments" (on H-N. Castaneda's symposium paper, "The Private-Language Argument"), *Knowledge and Experience: Proceedings of the 1962 Oberlin Colloquium in Philosophy*, C.D. Rollins, ed. (University of Pittsburgh Press), 106-118.

Chihara, C.S. and J.A. Fodor, "Operationalism and Ordinary Language: A Critique of Wittgenstein", *The American Philosophical Quarterly*, 2 (1965), 281-295.

Cook, John W., "Wittgenstein on Privacy", *The Philosophical Review*, 74 (1965), 281-314.

DeGrazia, Alfred, "The Scientific Reception System", *The American Behavioral Scientist*, 7 (1963), 38-55.

Feigl, Herbert, "Other Minds and the Egocentric Predicament", *The Journal of Philosophy*, 978-987 (1958), 55.

Garver, Newton, "Discussion: Wittgenstein on Private Language", *Philosophy and Phenomenological Research*, 20: March (1960), 389-396.

Garver, Newton, "Wittgenstein on Criteria", *Knowledge and Experience: Proceedings of the 1962 Oberlin Colloquium in Philosophy*, C.D. Rollins, ed. (University of Pittsburgh Press), 55-71.

Ginet, Carl, "Comments" (on Newton Garver's symposium paper, "Wittgenstein on Criteria"), *Knowledge and Experience: Proceedings of the 1962 Oberlin Colloquium in Philosophy*, C.D. Rollins, ed. (University of Pittsburgh Press), 72-80.

Hallie, Philip P., "Wittgenstein's Grammatical-Empirical Distinction", *The Journal of Philosophy*, 60: 565-578, (1963).

Hardin, C.C. "Wittgenstein on Private Languages", *The Journal of Philosophy*, 56: 868-882 (1959).

Hervey, Helen, "The Private Language Problem", *The Philosophical Quarterly*, 7 (1957), 63-79.

Malcolm, Norman, *Dreaming* (*Studies in Philosophical Psychology*, R.F. Holland, ed.) (London, Routledge and Kegan-Paul, 1959).

Malcolm, Norman, "Knowledge of Other Minds", *The Philosophy of Mind*, V.C. Chappell, ed. (Englewood Cliffs, N.J., Prentice-Hall, 1962), 151-159.

Malcolm, Norman, "Wittgenstein's *Philosophical Investigations*", *The Philosophy of Mind*, V.C. Chappell, ed. (Englewood Cliffs, N.J., Prentice-Hall, 1962), 74-100.

Medlin, Brian, "Critical Notice: *The Concept of a Person and Other Essays*" (by A.J. Ayer), *The Australasian Journal of Philosophy*, 42 (1964), 412-431.

Meiland, J.W., "Meaning, Identification and Other Minds", *The Australasian Journal of Philosophy*, 423 (1964), 360-374.

Moore, G.E., "Four Forms of Scepticism", *Philosophical Papers* (New York, The MacMillan Company, 1959), 196-226.

Mundle, C.W.K. "'Private Language' and Wittgenstein's Kind of Behaviorism", *Philosophical Quarterly*, 16 (1966), 35-46.

Peirce, Charles Saunders, "Some Consequences of Four Incapacities", *Values in a Universe of Chance: Selected Writings of Charles S. Peirce*, Philip P. Wiener, ed. (Garden City, New York, Doubleday and Company, 1958), 39-72.

Perkins, Moreland, "Two arguments against a Private Language", *Journal of Philosophy*, 62 (1965), 443-459.

Putnam, Hilary, "Dreaming and Depth Grammar", *Analytical Philosophy: First Series*, R.J. Butler, ed. (New York, Barnes and Noble, 1962), 211-235.

Putnam, Hilary, "Brains and Behavior", *Analytical Philosophy: Second Series*, R.J. Butler, ed. (Oxford, Basil Blackwell, 1965), 1-19.

Rhees, R. "Can There Be A Private Language?", *Aristotelian Society Supplementary Volume XXVIII* (London, Harrison and Sons, 1954), 77-94.

Richman, Robert J., "Concepts Without Criteria", *Theoria*, 31: 65-85, Part 2 (1965).

Richman, Robert J., "Why are Synthetic *A Priori* Judgments Necessary?", *Theoria*, 32: 5-20, Part I (1966).

Siegler, F.A., "Comments" (on Newton Garver's symposium paper, "Wittgenstein on Criteria"), *Knowledge and Experience: Proceedings of the 1962 Oberlin Colloquium in Philosophy*, C.D. Rollins, ed. (University of Pittsburgh Press), 77-80.

Stern, Kenneth, "Private Language and Skepticism", *The Journal of Philosophy*, 60 (1963), 745-759.

Stevenson, Charles L., "Some Relations Between Philosophy and the Study of Language", *Analysis*, 8: 1-9 (1947).

Stocker, Michael A.G., "Memory and the Private-Language Argument", *Philosophical Quarterly*, 16: (1966), 47-53.

Strawson, P.F. "Critical Notice: *Philosophical Investigations*" (by Ludwig Wittgenstein), *Mind*, 63: 70-99 (1954).

Strawson, P.F., *Individuals: An Essay in Descriptive Metaphysics* (London, Methuen, 1959).

Tanburn, N.P., "Private Languages Again", *Mind*, 72 (1963) 88-102.

Thomson, James F., "Comments" (on H-N. Castaneda's symposium paper, "The Private-Language Argument"), *Knowledge and Experience: Proceedings of the 1962 Oberlin Colloquium in Philosophy,* C.D. Rollins, ed. (University of Pittsburgh Press), 119-124.

Thomson, Judith Jarvis, "Private Languages", *The American Philosophical Quarterly,* 1 (1964) 20-31.

Todd, William, "Private Languages", *The Philosophical Quarterly,* 12(1962), 206-217.

Wellman, Carl, "Wittgenstein and The Egocentric Predicament", *Mind,* 68 (1959), 223-233.

Wellman, Carl, "Wittgenstein's Conception of a Criterion", *The Philosophical Review,* 71 (1962), 443-447.

Wittgenstein, Ludwig, *The Blue and Brown Books: Preliminary Studies for the "Philosophical Investigations"*, (Oxford, Basil Blackwell, 1958).

Wittgenstein, Ludwig, *Philosophical Investigations* (New York, The MacMillan Company, 1953).

Ziff, Paul, "Comments" (on Newton Garver's Symposium Paper, "Wittgenstein on Criteria"), *Knowledge and Experience: Proceedings of the 1962 Oberlin Colloquium in Philosophy*, C.D. Rollins, ed. (University of Pittsburgh Press), 61-86.

INDEX